The TEN Commandments

This booklet is not to be sold. It is a free educational service in the public interest, published by the Worldwide Church of God.

Printed in U.S.A.
Cover Illustration by Ren Wicks

ISBN 0-943093-37-6

Table of Contents

"THOU SHALT NOT"

OFTEN we hear the basic moral law impugned as negative and therefore outdated. Its Giver is often conceived as a stern, wrathful God, who angrily says to us: "THOU SHALT NOT!" It is sometimes looked upon as undesirable for modern, advanced, enlightened man. The Ten Commandments ought to be positive, they say, not negative.

Modern humanity looks upon itself as elevated to a plane of rational thinking, and with knowledge higher than God or God's law. Of course, when we understand, God's truth is the most positive religion or philosophy there is—it eradicates fear! It is the way of faith!

But is the negative form, "Thou shalt not," wrong for society today? Is it outmoded in building character? Should a perfect law be permissive, containing only dos and no don'ts?

Consider for a moment what is meant by true character.

Character—that is, true character—has been defined as: 1) coming to the knowledge of the true, as opposed to the false values—the right, instead of the wrong way; 2) making, of one's own free will and volition, the choice to do the right instead of the wrong; 3) the exercise of the will in actually doing the right instead of the wrong.

Character, then, once the true knowledge is acquired and the right decision made, involves self-discipline. The truly educated person is a self-disciplined person. What, then, does this self-discipline involve?

Two things: 1) self-restraint to resist the lower impulses and pulls of human nature—to restrain the self from desires, impulses, habits or customs that are contrary to the right way; and 2) self-propulsion or determined initiative to drive the self to do those things that ought to be done. In other words, in true character in action there is the positive and the negative.

Suppose one rejects the negative as faulty and something to be discarded altogether. Suppose one applies to the positive only and impels the self to do those positive things to be done, but exercises no restraint to resist those things of habit, impulse, desire or custom of others that ought not to be done. Because human nature is what it is, the very nature in such a one will pull constantly in the wrong direction. Thus character is destroyed. That person is out of balance, living in a hopelss world of permissiveness.

We find present in nature both the positive and the negative and the principle of opposites. Electricity involves both the positive and the negative. Some elements are alkaline; some are acid. Living things and beings in this world of matter are male and female. There are sins of both omission and commission.

Frequently we read the pitiful, feeble efforts of one who fancies in ignorant egotism that he or she is wiser than God, setting forth an idea of 10 positive commandments. Ten dos, and no don'ts. And what do we find? How much character would such a list of "commandments" produce?

Just about as much character as an electric light bulb would produce light with merely the one positive wire leading into it. Just about as much character as the male alone, without the female, could reproduce his kind. He might do a few good things, but all his good would be nullified and canceled out by the unrestrained evil he would commit.

No basic law of life, forming the basis of perfect character, could be a perfect law unless it contains, in perfect balance, both positive and negative.

The Ten Commandments, God's basic code, upon which all his laws, social, economic, civil and religious, hang are a perfect law (Ps. 19:7). It outlines, in broad detail, our right relationship with the true God that we may have all the needed guidance, help and blessings from God; and also our right relationship toward human neighbors—including parents, children, husband or wife. This law provides for every human need for our own good in a living, active, continuous relationship with the all-wise, all-powerful, all-loving God.

This perfect law forms the basis of all human relationships, as well as our God-relationship. It provides the wide, basic general rules affecting every phase of life:

a) Religious, in our relationship with God.

b) Family, in our relationship to parents, children, wife or husband, and is designed to preserve the blessed sanctity and dignity of the home;

c) Next-door and personal neighbors and friends;

d) Civil relationships—here are found the very basic civil laws respecting murder, larceny (theft), adultery, perjury;

e) Economic life—honesty, not coveting others' money, goods, property or possessions, which coveting is the very root source of today's economic principle of competition;

f) Social life—such commands as those respecting adultery, false witnessing, coveting, stealing, form the foundational principle of right social attitude and relationship with neighbors.

This law, in its basic principles, defines the whole duty of man (Eccl 12:13). It is the basis, in principle, for all the Bible. The entire Bible is, so far as its teaching is concerned, a magnification in specific detail of these basic principles.

This law contains, in brief summation-principle, all the positive and negative obligations of the perfect, rightly balanced life. It is the very antithesis of permissiveness! It expresses and reflects the very character of God.

The whole law is summed in one word, *love*. It is like God, for God is love, just as his law is love. It was given in love for us, and love is the fulfilling of the law—love in action.

It is love to God, and love to neighbor. It is perfect. It is complete.

THE FIRST COMMANDMENT

AND SO GOD spoke the Ten Commandments—revealing the laws of life which bring success and happiness and peace with God and with man. In this day of human reason, of agnosticism and of permissiveness, it is important to notice what the Almighty spoke first:

"And God spake all these words, saying, I am the Lord thy God, which have brought thee out of the land of Egypt, out of the house of bondage. *Thou shalt have no other gods before me*" (Ex. 20:1-3).

That is the first and, as we shall see later, greatest commandment.

"I am the Lord thy God" is a more revealing phrase than at first meets the eye.

The "I" who was speaking with such tremendous power was quite evidently the great Creator of heaven and earth. In His very manner of appearance, He had demonstrated His power as Creator by sending forth thunderings and lightnings and literally shaking Mount Sinai as if it were a wet dishrag!

The First Commandment and You

How, then, does the first commandment apply to YOU?

"I am the Lord thy God," the Creator states. *Is* the God of creation, the God of the Bible, really your God whom you serve and obey? Or have you conjured up your own false "god" or "gods"? Or are you falsely worshiping according to the "traditions of men," which Jesus said would cause you to worship God *in vain?* (Mark 7:7.)

These are things *you* need to consider!

God says that He is the one who has "brought thee out of the land of Egypt, out of the house of bondage." Throughout the Bible, ancient Egypt is used as a type of sin. All men and women are held in slavery to the organized system of this world, and to their own personal weaknesses.

When a person wants to change, God brings him *out* of that bondage—and he comes out willingly and gladly!

You need to examine whether or not you have ever really come out from the false traditions and ways of this world and have also repented of your own personal sins. God commands: "Thou shalt have no other gods before me." Have you put something else in place of God? Is your time, your interest, your service taken up more with something other than the true God? What idol have you placed between yourself and the true God, studying His Word, and living by it?

God says: "The heavens declare the glory of God; and the firmament showeth his handiwork" (Ps. 19:1). Throughout its pages, the Bible declares that God is the real Creator of this earth and of the universe. He is the one who gives life and breath to all creatures (Genesis 1).

Do you honestly think of God as your Creator and the one who gives you every breath of air you breathe? You should, for that is part of worshiping the true God and having no false gods before Him!

In the Bible, God is revealed not only as the Creator, but the one who sustains and who rules His creation—intervening in the affairs of His servants to guide and to bless and to deliver them.

David said: "The Lord is my rock, and my fortress, and my deliverer; my God, my strength, in whom I will trust; my buckler, and the horn of my salvation, and my high tower" (Ps. 18:2). Literally hundreds of times, David called upon God to intervene and deliver him from some trouble or calamity.

Do you go to God with these things, or do you trust in your own strength and in purely human devices?

What You Serve Is Your "God"

Most people think religion is something you do once a week in church—not realizing that it should affect every thought and word and action every day of your life! In everything you think or say or do, you either serve God, or else you serve your own lusts and Satan the devil!

The apostle Paul was inspired to explain this: "Know ye not, that to whom ye yield yourselves servants to obey, his servants ye are to whom ye obey; whether of sin unto death, or of obedience unto righteousness?" (Rom. 6:16.) There is no middle ground! You either delight in God and His law and serve and obey Him all day long, or else you serve and obey your own lusts!

One key to this situation is how you use your time. For your time is your life! The Bible commands us to be "redeeming [buying back] the time, because the days are evil" (Eph. 5:16). How much time do you actually spend each week studying and meditating on God's Word and law as David did? How much time do you spend in earnest, prevailing prayer to Almighty God? How much time do you spend in discussing the Bible with others who are interested, teaching it to your family, writing to others words of spiritual edification as well as words of purely social interest?

Now what is the most important thing God commands you to do?

When Jesus Christ was asked this question, He answered: "Thou shalt love the Lord thy God with all thy heart, and with all thy soul, and with all thy mind. This is the first and great commandment." Then Jesus continued: "And the second is like unto it, Thou shalt love thy neighbour as thyself. On these two commandments hang ALL the law and the prophets" (Matt. 22:37-40).

On these two commandments hangs the destiny of all nations and individuals! If men will obey these two commandments as they are magnified throughout the Bible, they will be blessed! If not, they will be cursed and will become wretched in their own confusion and frustration! As Jesus said, the very writings of the prophets hang on whether or not nations obey or disobey God's law. Every prophecy written against a nation shows that God foresaw that the nation would disobey and turn away its eyes from His law and obedience to His commandments!

These are the living laws—like the law of gravity—that rule the world in which you live!

Learn to Love and Worship God Above All Else

Jesus said the great commandment is to love God with all of your heart and soul and mind. You are to worship and serve God with all of your being!

Whenever you think or speak or hear of anything good or beautiful or wonderful, you should think of God! Remember James' inspired statement: "Every good gift and every perfect gift is from above, and cometh down from the Father of lights, with whom is no variableness, neither shadow of turning" (Jas. 1:17).

Whenever you find that God commands you in His Word to do something, you should not argue, "reason" or evade the issue, as so many falsely professing Christians do today.

Knowing that He made you and that your life really belongs to Him, you should present your body a living sacrifice as God tells you to do (Romans 12:1). You should serve and obey God with all your being—with a willing heart—and do all in your power to prepare yourself for and to further the work of reaching others with the message of the soon-coming government of God which will finally bring real peace to this earth.

Your attitude should always be that of Jesus Christ, your example, when He was called upon to give His very life: "Not my will, but thine, be done" (Luke 22:42).

This is what true worship really means! This is how to keep the first commandment, the GREAT commandment!

THE SECOND COMMANDMENT

IN His teaching in the Sermon on the Mount, Jesus stated: "Whosoever therefore shall break one of these *least* commandments, and shall teach men so, he shall be called the least in the kingdom of heaven: but whosoever shall *do* and *teach* them [even the *least* commandments], the same shall be called great in the kingdom of heaven" (Matt. 5:19).

Jesus was explaining and expounding and magnifying the Ten Commandments. He was showing that this spiritual law was a living law—like the law of gravity or inertia. When you break it, it breaks you!

When men or nations break the first commandment—"Thou shalt have no other gods before me"—they bring an inevitable penalty of suffering and wretchedness upon themselves and their posterity. Men cut themselves off from the source of their being, from the purpose of life, from the laws that would give them happiness, peace and joy. Men cut off from the true God are empty, frustrated and miserable.

Man is incomplete, then, having cut himself off from the true worship of the true God. Yet he is to worship that God alone: "Thou shalt have no other gods before me."

The second commandment tells us about how to worship the true God, what pitfalls to avoid in our worship, and of the continuing blessing or penalty that comes to our progeny as a result of the way in which we worship Almighty God.

The Second Commandment Stated

"Thou shalt not make unto thee any graven image, or any likeness of any thing that is in heaven above, or that is in the earth beneath, or that is in the water under the earth: Thou shalt not bow down thyself to them, nor serve them: for I the Lord thy God am a jealous God, visiting the iniquity of the fathers upon the children unto the third and fourth generation of them that hate me; and showing mercy unto thousands of them that love me, and keep my commandments" (Ex. 20:4-6).

The natural mind of physical man cries out for something to help him in his worship of God. He wants some physical object to "remind" him of the invisible God—some "aid" to worship. Yet, that is exactly what is forbidden in this commandment!

Jesus said: "But the hour cometh, and *now is,* when the true worshippers shall worship the Father in *spirit* and in *truth:* for the Father seeketh such to worship him" (John 4:23). Notice that it is only the "true" worshipers who are able to worship the Father in spirit and in truth. Many others attempt some form of worship but, because they limit their worship by a false concept of God, it is largely in vain. "God *is* a SPIRIT: and they that worship him *must* worship him in spirit and in truth" (verse 24).

The instant a man sets up any representation of God, he denies that which is essential in God. God is the essence of all power—all wisdom—all love. God is limitless. When man erects a mental or physical image of God, he automatically limits in his own thought and worship the God who will not be limited!

The Basis of Idolatry

Many times after reiterating the Ten Commandments, God again warned ancient Israel against any form of idolatry. "Ye shall make you no idols nor graven image, neither rear you up a standing image, neither shall ye set up any image of stone in your land, to bow down unto it: for I am the Lord your God" (Lev. 26:1). God was continually against *every* form of idol or image used in worship.

However, lest some misunderstand, let us pause at this point to note that God does *not* condemn art or sculpture, but rather the setting up of any picture or image or representation "to bow down unto it." In the original command in Exodus 20:4-6, God is *not* condemning every picture and image, but, as the command states, "Thou shalt not bow down thyself to them, nor serve them." So it is the use of art or sculpture as a form of worship or "aid" to worship that God condemns!

The real *basis* of all idolatry is that self-willed, rebellious man refuses to surrender himself to worship the true God *in the way that He commands!* Not really knowing the true God, then, nor having His Spirit, man thinks he needs some "aid" or "representation" to help him worship his humanly devised concept of God. Notice that this second commandment is not speaking of the worship of an *idol*—that's forbidden in the first commandment. This second commandment forbids the use of physical "aids" or "helps" in worshiping the invisible God.

A Converted Person Knows God

No man who really knows God as his Father—no man who is living in daily communion with Him—needs a picture or image to help him to pray. If a man thinks he needs this kind of help, it is simply because he has not come to know God—and undoubtedly is not filled with and led by the Holy Spirit of God.

In order to worship God in spirit, you must have the Holy Spirit. "Now if any man have not the Spirit of Christ, *he is none of his"* (Rom. 8:9).

But God gives His Holy Spirit only after genuine repentance and baptism—and only to those who "obey him" (Acts 2:38; 5:32).

Very few men in this day and age have truly surrendered themselves to obey God, to walk with Him, to let Him rule their every thought and word and action. Therefore, they are not actually acquainted with God. He seems far off—unreal—nebulous. They need a physical "reminder" in front of them to help them realize that He exists and is there to hear their prayers!

Pictures of Jesus

Thousands of professing Christians employ representations or pictures of a so-called Jesus Christ in their worship—and even display them in their homes. What does your Bible say about such pictures?

First of all, the second commandment itself obviously prohibits the use of anything which represents God or could easily become an object of worship. Certainly, since Jesus Christ is God (Hebrews 1:8), this would directly prohibit any picture or likeness of His person!

In addition, for those who might wish to "reason" or argue about this point, these so-called pictures of Christ have no similarity whatever to the way Jesus Christ really looked! Jesus—when in human flesh—was a Jew (Hebrews 7:14). The features in most of His supposed pictures are obviously not Jewish!

As the Word of God, Christ inspired the apostle Paul to write: "Doth not even nature itself teach you, that, if a man have long hair, it is a *shame* unto him?" (I Cor. 11:14.) Yet these pictures invariably show a man with long hair, soft features and a sentimental look in His eyes.

This is NOT the Christ of your Bible!

As a young man, Jesus was a carpenter—working outdoors. And He continued spending most of His time outdoors even during His ministry.

Jesus did not have beautiful, aristocratic features, but as He inspired Isaiah to describe His human appearance: "He hath no form nor comeliness; and when we shall see him, there is no beauty that we should desire him" (Isa. 53:2). As a human being, Jesus was a healthy young Jew in His early thirties, who with earnest conviction preached the message of God's soon-coming kingdom or rule over this earth.

However, if we think of Jesus' appearance at all, we should think, in general terms at least, of the way He looks today. He has described this for us in Revelation 1:14, 16: "His head and his hairs were white like wool, as white as snow; and his eyes were as a flame of fire . . . and his countenance was as the sun shineth in his strength."

As very God, Jesus' face now shines with radiance and

with power. As a human being, you would not dare to look directly into it!

If you use such false images or pictures of Christ, you are breaking the second commandment! And you are greatly limiting your concept of the living Christ—who now sits glorified at the right hand of God in heaven with His face shining like the sun in full strength!

Worshiping Systems and Institutions

One of the most common forms of modern idolatry is making an idol out of one's church or society. For many people, this world's society—its dictates, customs and traditions—becomes a literal god. Many people are desperately afraid of doing anything that might be regarded as different or "odd." They feel they must conform to this world and its ways.

But God commands: "Be NOT *conformed* to this world, but be ye transformed by the renewing of your mind" (Rom. 12:2). This command must seem very hard to obey for people who get to thinking that other *people* must be right in what they think and say and practice.

The Bible shows that many people in Jesus' day failed in their worship: "For they loved the praise of men more than the praise of God" (John 12:43). If you blindly obey the dictates of your family, your church or society instead of the direct commands of God, you are guilty of idolatry. That group or institution becomes an idol to you in place of the true God!

Even ritual in a church service is a dangerous thing, for however refined the ritual of some institutions may be, it begins and ends in the physical senses—and is not a valid substitute for the true worship of God "in spirit." The Bible directly warns that people of our day would have "a *form* of godliness, but [deny] the POWER thereof" (II Tim. 3:5).

The true God is the invisible, Eternal Creator and Ruler of the universe. How should you worship Him? He answers: "To this man will I look, even to him that is poor and of a contrite spirit, and trembleth at my word" (Isa. 66:2).

You must worship God directly—and with a humble and willing heart. You must study God's Word, willingly be corrected by it, and tremble before its authority over your life!

You need to pray to God in heaven on your knees and in silent prayer as you go about your daily tasks. You must come to know and love Him as your Father.

As Enoch and Noah and Abraham literally did, you must learn, figuratively, to "walk with God"—and be in constant and increasing communion and yieldedness to Him throughout every day of your life. Then—guided by His Spirit—you will never even begin to consider using an image or idol or picture as an "aid" to prayer and worship of the great sovereign Ruler of this universe, and your personal Father in heaven.

A Solemn Warning and Promise

We have seen that God forbids the making of any image or idol to represent Him: "For I the Lord thy God am a jealous God, visiting the iniquity of the fathers upon the children unto the third and fourth generation of them that hate me; and shewing mercy unto thousands of them that love me, and keep my commandments" (Ex. 20:5-6).

Because God is our Father, He is lovingly zealous for our eternal welfare. He is jealous over us, in that He will not countenance the worshiping of false gods by His children. This, of course, is for our own good!

If we persist in an idolatrous and vain form of worship, God says He will visit our iniquity upon our children and grandchildren and great-grandchildren. There are many ramifications to this statement and principle.

But there is one obvious direct meaning in this context. If, in worship, people put an idol, image or something else in place of God and come under the influence of that false worship, then they are not only harming themselves—but their children and grandchildren! The principle is that their false idea of worship will be transmitted to their children—damaging and wrecking their lives and happiness! It is a solemn and terrible thing thus to pass on to one's children a false concept of God. It is one of the most harmful things a parent can do!

But together with this warning, God gives a merciful promise to those who are willing to worship God as He commands. In their case, He is a loving and merciful God, "shewing mercy unto thousands of them that love me, and keep my commandments."

Here is a remarkable contrast. God only visits the iniquity of the fathers to the third and fourth generations before intervening with merciful punishment and awakening to truth. But He shows mercy unto the *thousandth* generation!

God calls men into His own immediate spiritual presence—to worship their Creator *directly*. Men can come to really *know* the great God of the universe as their personal Father. They can daily walk with Him, talk with Him. Whenever a man stops short of that face-to-face worship of the Eternal God, he is working ruin in his own character—breaking the commandment of God.

This is the meaning and force of the second commandment.

THE THIRD COMMANDMENT

Is God really first in your personal life? Does He come before anything else? People like to talk about religion and God, but they do not stand in awe of His position and His name.

And this spiritual cancer has within it the seeds of the destruction of our Western civilization!

The Third Commandment Stated

In discussing the first and second commandments, we found that we must guard against making a god out of *anything*— and putting it in place of the true God. And we learned that God commands us to worship Him *directly*—to walk with Him, to talk with Him, to really know and worship Him in spirit and truth—and to avoid using any image, picture or physical object as an "aid" to worship or to "remind" us of the great Creator.

The third commandment deals with God's name, His office, His position as the great sovereign Ruler of the universe: "Thou shalt not take the name of the Lord thy God in vain; for the Lord will not hold him guiltless that taketh his name in vain" (Ex. 20:7).

In the Bible, personal names have a meaning. The original Hebrew name of *Abram* was changed to *Abraham*—for Abraham means "a father of many nations." And Abraham was destined to become just that—"a father of many nations" (Gen. 17:5).

So it is with *God's name.*

God's Name Reveals the Kind of God You Worship

Every name or title of God reveals some attribute of the divine character. In studying God's Word, we learn new facts about God's nature and character with each new name by which He reveals Himself. In other words, God names Himself what He is!

If people use the *name* of God in a way which denies the true *meaning* and *character* of God, they are breaking the third commandment. God declares through Isaiah: "Hear ye this, O house of Jacob, which are called by the name of Israel, and are come forth out of the waters of Judah, which swear by the name of the Lord, and make mention of the God of Israel, but not in truth, nor in righteousness" (Isa 48:1). People to whom this prophecy applies use the name of God, but fail to obey the revelation of God contained in His name.

Many religious people repeat over and over the name of God in sermons or prayers. They are taking God's name *in vain*—to no good use or purpose!

The original command says: "The Lord will not hold him *guiltless* that taketh his name in vain." The Hebrew word here rendered "guiltless" may also be translated "clean": "The Lord will not hold him to be *clean* that taketh his name in vain." The test of spiritual cleanliness is the attitude of a man to the name of God! A man is clean or unclean according as he uses the name of God in truth—or for vanity. Do you realize what this means? It certainly indicates that a man is better off who—because of sincere religious doubts—has dropped the name of God from his vocabulary than is a professing Christian who talks about God continually, but denies Him in his daily life!

In the Lord's prayer, we are instructed to "hallow" God's name. And the third commandment with which we are dealing has directly to do with showing the proper respect for the name of God. One of the ten great points of God's eternal spiritual law is devoted to this very thing!

First of all, however, let us make it clear to those who

may have been misinformed on the subject that the third commandment does not refer to trying to speak God's name in the original Hebrew language!

The real importance of the name, of course, lies not in the phonetic sound which is used to describe God, but in the meaning which His names convey! Thus, one's name signifies one's office, authority and especially one's character. The names of God show us what God is like—they reveal His character!

Do you really know what God is like? Do you respect His various offices and His name as you should?

Turn to your Bible and check up!

God's Nature and Character Revealed

"In the beginning God created the heaven and the earth" (Gen. 1:1). In this very first verse of the Bible, God reveals Himself by the Hebrew name *Elohim.* There is one God—but more than one member in the Godhead, or God family! This same word *Elohim* is used in Genesis 1:26: "And *God [Elohim]* said, Let US make man in OUR image, after OUR likeness." Here it is clearly seen—in context with the passage itself—that more than one person shares the name of God—*Elohim.*

In the New Testament, this is made clear by the revelation that God created all things by and through Jesus Christ—who was with God and was God from the beginning (John 1:1-14; Ephesians 3:9). In these passages, therefore, it is revealed that God is more than one person—God and the "Word" or *Spokesman,* who later became Jesus Christ when born in human flesh. God is now a FAMILY. And the way the word *Elohim* is used in these early passages in Genesis and elsewhere certainly indicates that God is the creating kingdom or family! Interestingly, *Elohim* is plural in form but is used either in the singular or plural, depending on the context.

God, by virtue of being Creator, is also the Ruler over His creation. We find that immediately after creating the first man and woman, God gave them both a blessing and a command: "Be fruitful, and multiply, and replenish the earth, and subdue it" (Gen. 1:28). Yes, the true God is Ruler—and you should obey Him because He made you and gives you every breath of air you breathe!

In dealing with Abraham, God sometimes calls Himself *El Shaddai*, which means *"Almighty* God." So God is the source of *all* power! His name should be revered, because it stands for the one who is the source of all power, all might, and all authority.

The name most commonly translated "LORD" in the Old Testament is translated from the Hebrew letters YHWH, sometimes rendered *Yahweh*. The original Hebrew word means the "Eternal" or "Self-Existent One." The word is both used and defined in Genesis 21:33: "And Abraham planted a grove [tree—*eshel* in the Hebrew] in Beersheba, and called there on the name of the *Lord* [YHWH], the *everlasting* God." This Hebrew word, often translated "Jehovah" in some of the revised versions, shows God's character as the EVERLIVING God and is used to show His everlasting office in a covenant relationship to those whom He has created.

God has always existed and will always exist to carry out His blessings, His promises, and His covenant with His people! Our God is the *Eternal*—the Self-Existent One.

Throughout His Word, God's name is connected with His attributes—His power, His eternal existence, His mercy, His faithfulness, His wisdom, His love. Notice how the prophet David connects God's name with His creative power: "O Lord our Lord, how excellent is thy name in all the earth! who hast set thy glory above the heavens. . . . When I consider thy heavens, the work of thy fingers, the moon and the stars, which thou hast ordained; what is man, that thou art mindful of him? and the son of man, that thou visitest him?" (Ps. 8:1, 2-4.)

Here God is pictured as setting His glory above the heavens. Then David proceeds to show that God has created the heavens, the earth and man. No wonder God's name and office are to be respected!

In our everyday speech, many thoughtlessly misuse the very name of our Creator and our God! Men especially curse by using the name of the very One who gives us life and breath! Men—and even many women—give ready tongue to vile oaths—and often think they are proving their toughness or getting away with something by doing it! Using God's name carelessly in speech or in profanity is trifling with the name of our God.

God says: "To this man will I look, even to him that is poor and of a contrite spirit, and trembleth at my word" (Isa. 66:2). The very same thing may be said about the deep respect and godly fear we should have for God's name—which directly represents God's character, His Word and His purposes.

Should You Swear?

Many people today are accustomed not only to profane swearing and invoking God's name to back up their oaths, but also many legal ceremonies in some lands invoke the name of God in a form of swearing or an oath.

Jesus Christ said: "But I say unto you, Swear *not at all;* neither by heaven; for it is God's throne: nor by the earth; for it is his footstool: neither by Jerusalem; for it is the city of the great King" (Matt. 5:34-35).

God's name is so sacred and holy that we are commanded not to invoke it to back up our words or our oath! Fortunately, the American nation was founded by men who read their Bibles and made great allowance for religious liberty and freedom. Therefore, even though many public officials will, on occasion, ask you to raise your hand and "swear," they all realize that provision has been made so that you can employ the word "affirm" instead of swearing.

And actually, as we should all know, the simple affirmation or formal word of a God-fearing Christian is far more to be relied upon than ten thousand oaths given by a liar on the witness stand! The travesty of some few businessmen, politicians and even college professors taking God's name in vain on the witness stand in this manner bears ample proof of this statement!

Religious Titles to Avoid

Speaking of using certain expressions as a religious title, Christ said: "And call no man your *father* upon the earth: for one is your Father, which is in heaven" (Matt. 23:9). Although there is a flagrant and obvious abuse of this command, this statement of God's Word is clear to anyone who wishes to obey it.

Our only spiritual Father is God!

Of course, we *should* call our human parent "father," as God Himself does in the fifth commandment.

Another common misuse of the divine name is the application of the term "Reverend" to any human being—be he a minister or otherwise. For God applies this title to Himself alone: "He sent redemption unto his people: he hath commanded his covenant forever: *holy* and *reverend* is his [God's] name" (Ps. 111:9). "Reverend" applies to someone to be revered—someone worthy of worship! No mortal man is worthy of such a title! Even so great a servant of God as the apostle Paul himself was inspired to write: "For I know that in me (that is, in my flesh,) dwelleth no good thing" (Rom. 7:18). *Any* man who thinks he is worthy of worship—or deserves the title "Reverend"—is someday going to have to repent of breaking the third commandment!

The Most Common Sin of All

In teaching His disciples, and us as Christians, how to pray, Jesus Christ set forth the right manner to approach Almighty God and the attitude of reverence in which we should hold His office and His name. In the opening phrases of what is commonly called "The Lord's Prayer," our authorized translations of the Bible are most probably falsely punctuated. After the invocation, "Our Father which art in heaven"—the approach of man to God—there are three requests linked together, and then a clause following which conditions all three—and not the last one only. The correct rendering would be as follows: "Our Father which art in heaven, thy name be hallowed, thy kingdom come, thy will be done, as in heaven, so on earth." The phrase "as in heaven, so on earth" has reference not merely to "thy will be done," but to "thy kingdom come" and to "hallowed be thy name."

These thoughts contained in what is called the Lord's Prayer—the hallowing of God's name, the coming of His kingdom, and the doing of His will—are simply different phases of the same thing. For a man hallows God's name by submission to His kingdom and government, and by doing His will and obeying His laws.

Simply holding the phonetic sound of God's name in reverence is only a small part of fulfillment of the third commandment.

Jesus asked: "And why call ye me, Lord, Lord, and do not the things which I say?" (Luke 6:46.) Prayer without obedience is a subtle form of blasphemy!

Speaking of the religions of His day who refused complete obedience to the will and law of God, Jesus declared: "This people honoureth me with their lips, but their heart is *far from me.* Howbeit *in vain* do they worship me, teaching for doctrines the commandments of men" (Mark 7:6-7). In like manner, many today profess God with their lips, but their worship is vain!

"Not every one that saith unto me, Lord, Lord, shall enter into the kingdom of heaven; but he that *doeth the will* of my Father which is in heaven" (Matt. 7:21).

May God grant you the willingness to obey His will and law! May you learn to worship Him in spirit and in truth. May you learn to honor and reverence His great name—for it represents His creative power, His wisdom, His faithfulness, His love and kindness and patience and infinite mercy. It represents the character and office and dignity of the great God who sits at the controls of the universe!

THE FOURTH COMMANDMENT

WHY were you born? What is the meaning of your life? What is the true goal of life—and what are the laws of life by which that goal can be attained?

How much time do you spend each week in considering these most important questions? Most people are so busy with the day-to-day cares of making ends meet that they devote almost no time at all to the spiritual issues of life. If questioned about Bible study or prayer, most people reply that "there just isn't enough time" for these religious activities.

Yet people find time for television entertainment, the movies, parties and sports in the evenings and on weekends. God seems so far away. So we promise "to do better" someday.

The big question is—when? When will we take the time to really get to know God? When will we take time to study the Bible, to pray earnestly to the Creator as our Father, to meditate on the laws and purposes of life?

For most people, the true answer will probably be "never"—unless they learn to obey the fourth commandment of Almighty God! Obedience to this little-understood commandment is a powerful factor in bringing the lives of men and women close to the Creator God—and to His blessings and direct guidance.

The Test Commandment

The fourth commandment completes the first section of the Decalogue which deals with man's relationship to God. It provides for the perpetual observance of a sign of the relationship between God and man. "Remember the sabbath day, to keep it holy. Six days shalt thou labour, and do all thy work: but the seventh day is the sabbath of the Lord thy God: in it thou shalt not do any work, thou, nor thy son, nor thy daughter, thy manservant, nor thy maidservant, nor thy cattle, nor thy stranger that is within thy gates: for in six days the Lord made heaven and earth, the sea, and all that in them is, and rested the seventh day: wherefore the Lord blessed the sabbath day, and hallowed it" (Ex. 20:8-11).

This test commandment is, in its wording, the longest of any of the ten. It is placed, protectively as it were, in the very midst of the Ten Commandments. Yet, sad to say, it is the one command about which men "reason" and argue most and which they would most quickly tear asunder and try to separate from the rest of God's law.

Notice that it starts out with the injunction to "remember." This very statement proves that the Sabbath command was *already* understood by God's chosen people and that, in incorporating it as part of His covenant, God was *reminding* them of a spiritual command of which they already had knowledge.

"Remember the sabbath day, to *keep* it holy." You cannot "keep" cold water hot! And mortal *men* cannot make anything holy. Therefore, to fully grasp the significance of this divine command, we need to learn *who* made the Sabbath day holy and *when!*

Jesus said: "The sabbath was made for man, and not man for the sabbath: therefore the Son of man is Lord also of the sabbath" (Mark 2:27-28). Notice that Jesus said the Sabbath day was *"made."* Whatever was made has a Maker.

Note also that Jesus did not say that the Sabbath was made only for the Jewish people, but for MAN—for all mankind, in other words. Then He stated that He—Christ—is "Lord" of the Sabbath. In this statement, He claims to be—not the destroyer—but the *Lord* of the Sabbath. In His human life, Jesus kept the Sabbath, and many verses in the four Gospels are devoted to His instructions to the disciples in how it should be kept, and in freeing it from the traditions which the Jews had added.

But, before continuing, let us answer the question: "Who made the Sabbath day?"

Who Made the Sabbath?

In understanding the command to remember the Sabbath day and keep it holy, and in understanding who made the Sabbath in the first place, we need to turn to an account of the very beginning of God's creation. The New Testament gives such an account in the first chapter of the Gospel according to John. "In the beginning was the Word, and the Word was with God, and the Word was God. The same was in the beginning with God. *All things were made by him;* and without him was not any thing made that was made" (John 1:1-3). Here we find Jesus Christ described as the "Word" (or "Spokesman," as the original Greek may more properly be rendered).

The apostle Paul was inspired to speak of how God "created *all things* by Jesus Christ" (Eph. 3:9). In Hebrews, we find Christ described as the Son of God, "whom he hath appointed heir of all things, by whom also he made the worlds" (Heb. 1:2).

These and many other scriptures show that He was the person in the Godhead who later became Jesus Christ, who actually carried out the job of creation! He was the one who said: "Let there be light," and there *was* light. He was the one who created man—and set him on this earth in the garden of Eden.

So speaking of Him in particular who did the creating, the inspired writer of Genesis states: "And on the *seventh* day God ended his work which he had made; and he rested on the seventh day from all his work which he had made. *And God blessed the seventh day, and sanctified it:* because that in it he had rested from all his work which God created and made" (Gen. 2:2-3).

Jesus said that the Sabbath was made *for* man. Here we see that the Sabbath was made *when* man was made. And it was made *by* the very divine person who later became Jesus Christ! It was made as an intrinsic part of the environment which surrounded man and which God made in the seven days of creation. Notice that God "blessed" the *seventh* day and "sanctified" it. Such an honor was not conferred on any of the preceding six days. When God blesses something, He bestows His divine favor upon, and His divine presence in, that thing. The very word "sanctify" means to *set apart* for holy use or purpose. Thus, we see that in the very act of creation, the Almighty God put His divine favor upon, and set apart for holy use and purpose, a certain space of the most enduring thing there is—time.

The Sabbath Is a Blessing

Certainly this insight into the background of the Sabbath gives added meaning to God's command: *"Remember* the sabbath day, to *keep* it holy." Through Jesus Christ, God made the seventh day of the week holy—and on His authority as our Creator He commands us to keep it that way!

The Sabbath, then, is holy time. Yet it was made *for* man—as a great blessing to all mankind!

Our Creator knew that we would need a period of rest and worship every seventh day, and this is the basic purpose for which the Sabbath was created. Each of us tends to become overly absorbed in our daily cares and work and pleasure during the week. Our Creator foresaw this, and set apart His Sabbath day as a consecrated time when we can completely forget our daily routine and draw closer to the Creator God in study, meditation and prayer. Modern man desperately needs this period of time in which to have real communion with his Maker and God. Taking time to think about God and to worship Him, to pray, to study and meditate upon the purpose for human existence, and upon God's revealed laws of life—all this adds great strength and meaning to man's life the other six days of the week.

The Sabbath is one of the greatest blessings that has ever been bestowed upon the human family!

The Command Expounded

Understanding that the Sabbath command is just as binding

as the commandments against murder and adultery, let us proceed to analyze and expound this commandment of God and its application to our personal lives today.

Except for the explanatory and expository statements, the fourth commandment consists of two basic injunctions: First, "Remember the sabbath day, to keep it holy." Second, "Six days shalt thou labour, and do all thy work."

It is by the authority of God that the first six days of the week are appointed for man's business and labor. It is the will of God that man should work and earn his daily bread. He who idles away his time in the six days is equally guilty in the sight of God as the one who works on the seventh! The idle person is ordinarily clothed with rags, and his idle mind and hands lead him into many wretched vices and sins.

This second part of the Sabbath command is just as binding as the first! He who never works is totally unfitted for worship! The honest, purposeful work of the six days is in itself an act of worship and obedience to God.

Man is placed in a world that contains all that is necessary for his physical being, but to obtain it he must work! It is part of the original intention of God, for man was placed in the garden of Eden "to dress it and to keep it" (Gen. 2:15).

However, in like manner, he who never pauses from his daily business and pursuits to worship as God has commanded on the seventh day, which God has made holy and set apart, is—through lack of contact with his Maker—rendered incapable of his highest potential achievement in work, in service and in the joy of accomplishment.

Since the very Creator has so commanded, we can keep the Sabbath day of rest and spiritual rejuvenation with complete confidence that God will bless and prosper us because we have done this!

A Paid Vacation

Normally speaking, if you would quit working every few days to take a needed rest, you might naturally expect to get behind with your work and finances. But God Himself has set in motion a great law. God's Ten Commandments are living, active laws—just like the law of gravity. They are in operation—they work automatically. The law of the Sabbath—

backed up by the very power of the Creator—says that if you will pause to rest and worship Almighty God on the seventh day every week, you will be so blessed during the work of the six days that this will more than make up for what you might have accomplished by laboring on God's Sabbath! Do you realize what this amounts to? In one way of looking at it, God is giving us a paid vacation every seventh day!

But this vacation is not only for the purpose of physical rest, it is also a time for worship, for spiritual rededication, for the contemplation and exercise of the spiritual purposes and laws of life which God has set. In the observance of the seventh day which God has made holy—and which alone points to creation—man is brought into close communion with his Maker and his God. For God's very presence as well as His divine blessing are especially evident in this day which He has set apart and sanctified.

These are the busiest days that humanity has ever seen. These are days in which most men seem to have little or no time for the contemplation of the spiritual purposes and goals of life—the most important questions which man ought to be considering.

The tremendous blessing of God's true Sabbath is that it enables man to take time to fully consider and weigh these most important of all questions in life—and to commune with his God and Creator in a way in which few men in this age have ever experienced. The true observance of the Sabbath would keep man in contact with God! Without that contact, he is cut off from the very purpose of his existence, from the laws that govern his success or failure in life, from an understanding of what he is, where he is going and how to get there. Without this contact with the Creator God, the life of man is emptiness, frustration and a thing of vanity. In this age above all others, man needs the contact with God, the spiritual strength and understanding, and the divine blessing and guidance which proper observance of God's true Sabbath provides.

Jesus' Example

Jesus Christ—the inspired example of how every true Christian ought to live—taught by His own life and actions that the Sabbath is a holy convocation (commanded assembly) for God's people as is taught in Leviticus 23:3. Jesus' example and customary practice is recorded in Luke 4:16, where we read that Jesus, "as his custom was . . . went into the synagogue on the sabbath day, and stood up for to read."

Certainly the true Sabbath is a day for the united worship and adoration of God by His called servants. And it is a time for the preaching and expounding of God's Word and His living laws. It is the duty of every true Christian, then, to find out where that Church is in which he can really worship God "in spirit and in truth," a Church which properly observes the true Sabbath of the Creator God, and a Church in which man is taught to "live by *every* word of God."

You need to find out about this Church. Write for the informative *free* booklet *Where Is the True Church?* We also offer you personal services to help you understand where God's Church is and to help you with any questions you may have.

Rejoice in God's Sabbath

Learn to keep the Sabbath in a positive way! Use the seventh day that God has sanctified and made holy as He has intended—to rest from worldly labor, to pray, to study and to meditate on God's Word and the purpose for human existence. Take time to do good to others, to care for the sick, to visit the afflicted. Assemble with other true Christians on the Sabbath if this is possible.

The seventh day and that day alone which God made holy is the commanded and God-blessed time for rest, for worship and for contemplation of the vital keys to the meaning of life.

If you have any doubt whatsoever on which day the Sabbath should be observed, write for our free, fully illustrated booklet *Which Day Is the Christian Sabbath?*

Properly understood and properly observed, the fourth commandment—the keeping of God's holy Sabbath—is one of the greatest blessings that the Creator has ever bestowed upon the children of men! It is an identifying sign between man and the true God. Remember it—keep it holy!

THE FIFTH COMMANDMENT

YOUTHFUL violence and insolence characterize the age in which we live.

The source of the problem? A lack of deep-seated respect for constituted authority beginning in infancy and continuing throughout life.

This problem has its origin in childhood—in the home! Long before a child is even aware of the existence of the church, the school, the nation, he is forming attitudes and habits toward those who are his superiors in the nursery, the home, and the neighborhood. Developed from infancy, this part of a child's character will undoubtedly affect his thoughts and actions for the rest of his natural life!

The first four commandments define man's relationship with God. They teach us the magnitude of God's power and name—and exhort us to remember Him as Creator of all that is.

The fifth commandment is placed first among those which govern our human relationships. It is not only chief in importance among these, when we understand its full meaning, but it acts as a "bridge" between the two sections of God's law. For true obedience to the fifth commandment is inevitably linked with obedience and honor toward God Himself! Our Creator knew this when He inspired it to be "the first commandment with promise."

The Fifth Commandment Stated

"Honour thy father and thy mother: that thy days may be long upon the land which the Lord thy God giveth thee" (Ex. 20:12).

Why honor our parents?

The true answer reveals the depth of this commandment and its true import. If only every parent on earth might come to realize the tremendous influence upon a child's later life that automatically comes as a direct result of obedience or disobedience to this God-given command!

This commandment is one of the ten great points of God's eternal, spiritual law. Under the Old Testament dispensation, the penalty for directly and flagrantly violating this law was death! "He that smiteth his father, or his mother, shall be surely put to death.... And he that curseth his father, or his mother, shall surely be put to death" (Ex. 21:15, 17). That is how important this command is in God's eyes!

The home and the family unit are the basis of all decent society. And the relationship of children to their parents is an exact type of the spiritual relationship between true Christians and God. The lessons of character learned in that relationship may last children the rest of their lives—and for eternity!

In the eyes of a small child, a parent stands in the place of God Himself. For the loving and affectionate parent is the child's provider, protector, teacher and lawgiver. A child's early training and response to this relationship will in large measure determine his later response to the larger relationships with society. And, ultimately, it is certain to affect his relationship with his spiritual Father in heaven.

Honor and Respect for Parents

The New Testament magnifies this command in many places. The apostle Paul wrote: "Children, obey your parents in the Lord: for this is right. Honour thy father and mother; (which is the first commandment with promise)" (Eph. 6:1-2). The original command to honor father and mother applies to all of us throughout our lives. But in this place children specifically are told to obey their parents "in the Lord."

Because of his total lack of experience and judgment, it is absolutely necessary that a child be taught to obey his parents instantly and without question. Explanations and reasons for this may and should be given to the child from time to time. But, at the moment a parental command is given, there may not be time or opportunity to give the reason why!

Therefore it is imperative that a child be taught the habit of unquestioning obedience to his parents. For, until the young child develops, his parents stand to him in the place of God. And God holds them responsible for teaching and directing the child properly.

Obedience "in the Lord"

By direct implication, a parent is bound by the fifth commandment to make himself honorable. For to be honored, one must be honorable. Every parent needs to realize that he represents God to his child! He should live a life worthy of the child's deep respect and reverence. Then he should teach his child to honor and respect both of his parents.

As the child matures, the parent should instruct his child about the existence of the great spiritual Father of all life, the Creator of heaven and earth, the sovereign Ruler of the universe—Almighty God.

Christian parents should teach their children to honor and obey their spiritual Father with even more implicit faith and love than they do their earthly parents. For the greatest lesson that a child or anyone can be taught is that of fear and obedience to the One who set in motion all life in the first place! Thus, a child will be taught the habit of obedience. He will learn to respect authority. In due time, when his mind is opened to know the Supreme Father of all life, he will already have learned the very basis of God's character—loving obedience to God, and deep respect and reverence for all law and constituted authority.

Blessing for Obedience

The apostle Paul reemphasizes the blessing attached to the fifth commandment: "That it may be well with thee, and thou mayest live long on the earth" (Eph. 6:3). Obedience to the fifth commandment automatically results in the building of habits and character which tend to long life. A young person so trained will avoid the recklessness, the violence, the wrong companionships and the rebellion against authority which often result in untimely death. And, in its ultimate meaning, those who learn to respect and obey their parents and later—because of this training—God Himself, will certainly "live long on the earth." For, as Jesus said: "Blessed are the meek [the humble and obedient]: for they shall inherit the earth" (Matt. 5:5).

There are also many everyday blessings to the obedient child. Certainly not the least of these is a sense of security. A child is confused unless he is told the bounds of his activities. But if a child is told what those bounds are by his parents—and stays within them—he is then relieved of the responsibility which he innately realizes his parents must shoulder.

Frustration is another problem which is alleviated. The disobedient child is a frustrated child—for his mind is constantly plagued with feelings of guilt and rebellion. A child who loves, honors and obeys his parents is a blessed child indeed. He will tend to live a more truly happy, carefree and purposeful life. And in his spiritual life, he will pass through the natural and beautiful sequence from the honoring of his parents to the joyful worshiping of his God!

Thus far we have dealt primarily with the application of the fifth commandment to children and young people. But the original command to "honor" our parents is not addressed to children—but to everyone.

Even Adults Should Honor Their Parents

The time may come when it is no longer necessary or right that a person should strictly obey his parents. But the day should never come when he ceases to honor them. The word "honor" has a much larger meaning than that of obedience. It indicates a high respect, as for worth, merit or rank. It denotes a feeling of high esteem and reverence.

A person who has properly obeyed his parents in childhood later expresses his honor for them in a deeper appreciation of the comforts and training they provided him as a child. This honor expresses itself in courtesy, thoughtfulness and kind deeds.

As we mature, it becomes increasingly evident that untold hours of work, of anxious thought and agonized prayer were bestowed for our welfare by faithful and loving parents. It should become the delight of every decent man and woman to return this love which our parents showered on us.

In the evening of life, many parents long for this affection and fellowship with their children more, perhaps, than for any other blessing. Let us think and act on this opportunity to return the love our parents so freely gave!

To the everlasting shame of our professing Christian society, thousands of elderly parents are reduced to living on a mere pittance that comes to them through governmental agencies. In all too many cases, the children are able but simply unwilling to provide additional comforts for their parents.

Jesus Christ gave one of the most forceful interpretations of the fifth commandment in its application to this very problem. In His day, men were excusing themselves from providing for the necessities of their parents. They were saying that funds which might have been used in this way were "Corban"—that is, dedicated to the service of the altar. These funds were not part of God's tithe, but rather an additional offering which was used to gain favor in approaching God. Reproaching these hypocritical religionists, Jesus said: "Full well ye reject the commandment of God, that ye may keep your own tradition. For Moses said, Honour thy father and thy mother; and, Whoso curseth father or mother, let him die the death" (Mark 7:9-10).

Now notice how these hypocrites "reasoned" their way around this commandment! Jesus continued: "But ye say, If a man shall say to his father or mother, It is Corban, that is to say, a gift, by whatsoever thou mightest be profited by me; he shall be free. And ye suffer him no more to do ought for his father or his mother; making the word of God of none effect through your tradition . . ." (verses 11-13).

Jesus condemned these hypocrites. His words plainly teach that a Christian must give material and financial assistance to his aged parents if it is possible and their needs so require. He must not excuse himself by saying that all his extra funds are "dedicated to God"! This is a part of our obedience to the fifth commandment.

Jesus' Own Personal Example

Jesus Christ LIVED the message He taught. His own personal life is a dramatic illustration of *obedience* to the fifth commandment.

Just before His death, Jesus said: "I have kept my Father's commandments" (John 15:10). Through obedience to His heavenly Father, and to his human parents as well, Jesus grew in wisdom and maturity even as a youth.

Even in His dying moments, while suffering one of the most agonizing deaths ever devised by men, Jesus honored and loved His mother to the very end. Just before He died on the stake, John records: "When Jesus therefore saw his mother, and the disciple standing by, whom he loved, he saith unto his mother, Woman, behold thy son! Then saith he to the disciple, Behold thy mother! And from that hour that disciple took her unto his own home" (John 19:26-27).

Here Jesus made final provision for His mother to be taken care of by John after His death. At a time when the thoughts of all other men would have been of *self,* Jesus still remembered the fifth commandment and extended love and honor to the woman who bore Him, who nourished Him from infancy, who taught Him from the Scriptures, and who now stood in this awful place—unashamed—weeping at His death.

Remember the *perfect example* of Jesus Christ! "Honour thy father and thy mother: that thy days may be long upon the land which the Lord thy God giveth thee."

THE SIXTH COMMANDMENT

THIS is an age of hate and violence. It is an age of intense competition, strife and personal tensions.

The nations of the earth—and the individuals within them—are conditioning their minds and consciences to the likelihood of wholesale murder—and possibly world suicide. Naturally, this situation is devastating to the spiritual principles and ideals of all peoples. The effect of this is being felt now—even as you read this booklet.

We have seen the blessings that come through awe and respect for the one true God, through reverencing His name and office, through hallowing His Sabbath day and keeping it in the true knowledge of Him, and through honoring our fathers and mothers in their high office which directly reflects God's Fatherhood and love for all creation. In all these commandments, we have seen love and wisdom and blessings. And so it is with the sixth commandment.

Amid the thunder and lightning and literal shaking of Mount Sinai, God's voice *thundered* the sixth commandment: "Thou shalt not murder" (Ex. 20:13, Jewish Publication Society translation). Biblical authorities agree that "murder" is a more correct reading of the original inspired Hebrew than the word "kill." For it is possible to kill and yet not to murder. And it is important to understand that only the letter of God's law was given to ancient Israel, whereas

Christians are to live by the spirit and fullest intent of that law as magnified by Christ Himself.

Under the original letter of the law, it was intentional killing or murder which was forbidden. Remember that in this same "book of the covenant" given to Israel, God commanded them to kill or execute those guilty of major crimes (Ex. 21:12-17). Also, the instructions in Numbers 35:9-34 show that accidental killing was not regarded as murder. Even here, though, manslaughter was obviously a terrible offense—and the careless or unwitting slayer had to remain in a city of refuge for perhaps many years until the high priest died.

Just as capital punishment was commanded by God for serious crimes under the letter of the law, so the commanded wars of Israel should be viewed not as acts of wholesale murder but the carrying out of the divine will through human instruments. Notice in Deuteronomy 7:1-2 that God directly commanded Israel to exterminate the heathen tribes in the land of Canaan. This was not humanly devised warfare nor was it personal vengeance or malice. It was the express will of Almighty God who gives life—and who alone has the right to say when it shall be taken.

Incidentally, it should be noted that the history of the time indicates that these nations occupying Canaan were absolutely wicked in the extreme—and were burning alive their own children in human sacrifice to their pagan gods. This was part of the intelligent reason why the Creator ordered their extermination at that time. Notice that in all these cases where God permitted man to take life, it was only as His agent—at His express will.

God's original purpose was that man should learn not to kill. And although it was permitted in certain instances to the carnal, unconverted people of Israel, we shall see that God is now developing in His Spirit-begotten children the character to *love,* to serve and to save life—not to destroy it.

The Source of Life

"And God said, Let us make man in *our image,* after *our likeness:* and let them have *dominion . . .*" (Gen. 1:26). Man is given life by his Creator. He did not give it to himself.

Neither may he take it from himself—or from others. Life is sacred because it is God-given. Man has been made in the very image and likeness of God. Of all the physical creation, only man has the type of mind that God possesses. God is the Ruler of all that is. But out of human flesh He is forming literal sons who will someday share in that rule. So God said: "Let them have dominion. . . ."

Man needs experience in order to develop the character God purposes for him. Experience requires time. And a man's life consists of just so much time. God gave that life for the supreme purpose of preparing another son to be in His kingdom and family forever.

The giving of life and breath and ability includes all. It is the most wonderful gift of which physical man has knowledge. The taking of life ends all. It cruelly and unexpectedly crushes all the hopes and dreams and plans of a man made in the very image of the Creator Himself. It is a wicked usurpation by man of a prerogative belonging to God alone who gives life in the first place—and who alone has the authority to take it away (Job 1:21). That is why *any* form of murder is one of the ten great sins. It is destroying the highest creation of Almighty God! In effect, it is an attempt to thwart the very purpose of the great sovereign Ruler of the universe! The Giver of all life is God. And puny, mortal man has no business interfering with God's *greatest gift!*

Personal Application of the Commandment

Jesus Christ came into this world to "magnify" God's law and "make it honorable" (Isa. 42:21). Jesus cast a spotlight, as it were, on the Ten Commandments, and showed their real spiritual intent and meaning in the full Christian life. Jesus said: "Ye have heard that it was said by them of old time, Thou shalt not kill; and whosoever shall kill shall be in danger of the judgment: *but I say unto you,* That whosoever is angry with his brother without a cause shall be in danger of the judgment . . ." (Matt. 5:21-22).

Here murder is traced to its source—hate and anger. Christ declared that if personal anger fills the heart of one of His subjects, such a person is in danger of judgment.

This is Jesus Christ's application of the sixth commandment to you and me. If we harbor hate and anger in our hearts, we are harboring the spirit of murder. Action follows thought. First we think, then we do! The Spirit of Christ guides us not only to control our actions, but to control our thoughts and our attitudes. In part, the New Covenant is the process of God writing His law in our hearts and minds (Hebrews 8:10).

God spoke through Paul: "Dearly beloved, avenge NOT yourselves, but rather give place unto wrath: for it is written, Vengeance is mine; I will repay, saith the Lord" (Rom. 12:19). Man is incapable of taking vengeance with proper wisdom and justice for all concerned. God alone has the wisdom and power and the right to take vengeance on human beings—to the extent of executing them if need be. The true Christian must learn that God is real—and that His protection and His vengeance are just as real!

How, then, should you deal with your enemies? "Therefore if thine enemy hunger, feed him; if he thirst, give him drink: for in so doing thou shalt heap coals of fire on his head. Be not overcome of evil, but overcome evil with good" (verses 20-21).

It takes real strength of character to help and serve your fellow human being when he has directly tried to harm you! It takes the spiritual wisdom to realize that he is a fellow human being, made in the image of God, and simply misguided for the time being in his thoughts and actions.

Humanity's Greatest Crime

Perhaps the greatest international crime of humanity is the scourge of war. Millions of human lives created in the image of God have been mercilessly slaughtered down through the ages in useless, senseless, idiotic wars which in most cases failed utterly to accomplish their stated purpose!

The spirit of God's law as magnified by Jesus Christ is totally opposed to every form of war! Nearly all the really great religious and political leaders of the world have acknowledged the utter futility of war. Before the outbreak of World War II, Pope Pius XII declared: "Everything is gained by peace; nothing is gained by war." One of the most respected statesmen and military leaders of our time, General

Douglas MacArthur, stated: "Men since the beginning of time have sought peace . . . military alliances, balances of powers, leagues of nations, all in turn failed, leaving the only path to be by way of the crucible of war. The utter destructiveness of war now blots out this alternative. We have had our last chance. If we will not devise some greater and equitable system, our Armageddon will be at our door. The problem basically is theological and involves a spiritual recrudescence, an improvement of human character that will synchronize with our almost matchless advances in science, art, literature, and all material and cultural developments of the past two thousand years. It must be of the spirit if we are to save the flesh."

The greatest statesman of all times was Jesus Christ. He was the Spokesman for the government or kingdom of God. Christ said: "Ye have heard that it hath been said, Thou shalt love thy neighbour, and hate thine enemy. But I say unto you, *Love your enemies,* bless them that curse you, do good to them that hate you, and pray for them which despitefully use you, and persecute you" (Matt. 5:43-44).

There is a great deal of highly respectable, cultured and educated paganism abroad in the world today under the name of "Christianity." But can even this sophisticated paganism face these clear words of Jesus Christ without confessing that His life, His teaching, and His Spirit condemn the very essence of war? More lives have been snuffed out prematurely, more suffering has been endured, more homes have been wrecked and broken, more time and property has been utterly wasted because of the scourge of war than through any other means in the history of man! And war has never solved the problems of men or brought permanent peace. Instead, it only breeds more war! "For all they that take the sword shall *perish* with the sword" (Matt. 26:52).

The Bible Teaching

Jesus Christ came into this world as a messenger of the government or kingdom of God. He took no part in this world's politics or wars. On trial for His very life before Pontius Pilate, He said: "My kingdom is not of this world: if my kingdom were of this world, then would my servants fight, that I should not be delivered to the Jews: but now is my kingdom not from hence" (John 18:36).

As we have stated, only God who gave life has the right to take life. Therefore, only God has the right to wage war! And, as Jesus taught, God does not choose to have His children wage war for Him during this age.

Jesus said that His servants would fight if His kingdom were of this world. But it is not.

Through the apostle James, God shows that war results from a type of spirit exactly opposite that which He wants His servants to have. "From whence come wars and fightings among you? come they not hence, even of your lusts that war in your members? Ye lust, and have not: ye kill, and desire to have, and cannot obtain: ye fight and war, yet ye have not, because ye ask not" (Jas. 4:1-2).

God's Government Will End War

Jesus Christ came preaching the good news of the government or rule of God. That rule is based on the Ten Commandments—God's spiritual law. Jesus magnified that law and showed its spiritual intent and purpose. He taught that if we even hate our brother, we are spiritually guilty of murder! Jesus taught that men should obey the laws of God and prepare for His coming kingdom by yielding themselves to let God's laws—His character—be placed within them.

When God's government does come to this earth, His law will go forth as the standard of conduct of all nations (Micah 4:1-2). At that time, God will punish rebellious nations in perfect wisdom and justice. As for the peoples of the world themselves? "Nation shall not lift up a sword against nation, neither shall they learn war any more" (verse 3).

War involves learning to hate and kill. Young men will no longer be forced to learn an attitude which is diametrically opposed to the rule of God's law of love.

Jesus Christ is against the spirit of murder in every form. He is against war—and someday He will put an end to it forever! He is against all malice and envy and hate.

And the great Father of Jesus Christ, who governs the universe from His throne in heaven—that God thunders at an age of violence and rebellion: "Thou shalt not murder."

THE SEVENTH COMMANDMENT

IS "SEXUAL COMPATIBILITY" the all-important thing in marriage? In this age of broken homes, juvenile delinquency and modern psychology, many will say that the answer is "yes."

But the fact remains that the more "modern" theories about marriage are put into practice, the faster the divorce rate climbs and the more little children are doomed to grow up without the blessing of a stable, happy home. Something is painfully wrong when so many marriages end in the divorce courts.

The marriages end—but the suffering and anguish and grief do not. For the little children of such broken homes, the years of frustration and emptiness are only beginning.

Is there a real meaning to marriage that modern man needs to understand? Are there God-given laws and principles that can safeguard a Christian marriage and make it happy and purposeful?

The Seventh Commandment Stated

The Creator God devoted two of His ten great spiritual laws—the Ten Commandments—to protecting the relationships in the home and family. In this booklet, we have already discussed the first of these: "Honour thy father and thy mother."

The other law directly governing the home and family is contained in the seventh commandment: "Thou shalt not commit adultery" (Ex. 20:14). Almighty God gave this commandment to protect the honor and sanctity of marriage. Immediately after the sixth command, which declares the sacredness of human life, God gives this law to safeguard the highest earthly relationship. For marriage and the home are the basis of all decent society. The words of the command directly forbid adultery as violating the sacred rights of the marriage relation. Its spirit makes evident the fact that all unchaste conduct before marriage is a wrong done to the future marriage, and unfaithfulness before marriage is violating the command as much as adultery committed after marriage.

In this permissive modern age, it is important to remind ourselves that God has promised to reward those who break this commandment with the penalty of death. "And the man that committeth adultery with another man's wife, even he that committeth adultery with his neighbour's wife, the adulterer and the adulteress shall surely be *put to death*" (Lev. 20:10). The seventh commandment also covers in principle all other forms of illicit sex, including male and female homosexuality—now an *enormous sin* in the Western world—which also warranted the death penalty (Lev. 20:13).

Again, in the New Testament, God says: "For the wages of sin is DEATH" (Rom. 6:23).

Why is the sin of adultery so great as to merit death, and, in God's judgment, eternal death in the lake of fire—unless really repented of? The answer is this: Marriage is in God's sight such a precious, righteous, holy thing that it must not be defiled! The meaning of marriage and its great purpose in God's plan needs *desperately* to be understood in this age of unhappy marriages and broken homes.

The Purpose of Marriage

It is impossible to understand the true meaning of marriage without first understanding that sex and marriage are God-given and God-ordained. To leave God out of the picture—as this modern age is doing—is to degrade the marriage union to mere animalism. Notice *God's* purpose in creating man and woman! "And the Lord God said [after He had made only the man], It is not good that the man should be alone; I will make an help meet for him" (Gen. 2:18). God saw that man was incomplete by himself, and so He decided to make a help "meet" or *suitable* for the man—one with whom man could really share his life.

So the first and primary purpose of marriage is to make man and woman complete. Each is incomplete without the other. Man alone was not able to fulfill the purpose for which God created him—was not able to learn the lessons of character which God intended—and so God created the woman as a "help" to the man. And, in the very creation, God showed that they were to dwell together as man and wife in one fleshly union—to share everything in this life, and so make their lives meaningful and complete in a physical sense at least.

The second purpose of sex and marriage is the begettal and training of children. For God had told the man and woman: "Be fruitful, and multiply, and replenish the earth, and subdue it . . ." (Gen. 1:28).

With begetting children comes the responsibility of protecting and training them. A stable, happy home and marriage are indispensable to the correct nurture and training of a child. And God commands: "Train up a child in the way he should go: and when he is old, he will not depart from it" (Prov. 22:6).

The home and family are the basis of all decent society! The lessons of character learned in the home—patience, understanding, kindness—all of these are qualities that God wants in man for all eternity; and the family relationship is one of the best places in which they can be learned!

Better than in any other place, the lessons of decency, loyalty, and a sense of responsibility are learned in a happy and well-balanced home.

And so, in addition to making man complete and the begetting and training of children, a third great purpose in sex and marriage is the building of character in the home and family relationship. The kingdom and law of God are based on love. Jesus said: "It is more blessed to give than to receive" (Acts 20:35). To obey God's law of marriage, man and wife must literally give themselves to each other in every phase and facet of their lives.

Marriage Pictures Christ and His Church

As ordained by God, the marriage union is a holy thing. It is so holy that in His Word Almighty God uses the marriage union as a type of the relationship between Christ and His Church! Notice Ephesians 5:22-24: "Wives, submit yourselves unto your own husbands, as unto the Lord. For the husband is the head of the wife, *even as* Christ is the head of the church: and he is the saviour of the body. Therefore as the church is subject unto Christ, so let the wives be to their own husbands in every thing."

In this place, God shows that in the Christian home the wife is to submit herself to her husband as the head of that home, just as she must learn to submit to Christ Himself for all eternity! In this holy relationship, she is learning a lesson of lasting faithfulness!

Then the husbands are addressed: "Husbands, *love* your wives, even as Christ also loved the church, and gave himself for it.... So ought men to love their wives as their own bodies. He that loveth his wife loveth himself" (verses 25, 28).

Jesus Christ served, helped, trained, protected and eventually gave Himself for His Church. So are husbands to protect, to provide for, to guide, to encourage, to love and give to their wives! A Christian man is to be the head of his house. Yet he is to use that office to serve and to give protection, guidance and happiness to his wife and family. And Almighty God holds him responsible for being the right kind of head!

Because of this great lesson and purpose in marriage, God says: "For this cause shall a man leave his father and mother, and shall be joined unto his wife, and they two shall be one flesh" (verse 31). In the marriage union, man and woman are made one. Their relationship is then to picture the eternal, loving and serving relationship of Christ and His Church. Therefore, nothing should come between them. The lesson of marriage is to teach us eternal faithfulness to Jesus Christ as our Head! To separate from one's God-given mate is to fail to learn the lesson which God intends for us to learn in marriage. It is a reproach to Almighty God—for it denies His wisdom in ordaining the marriage union in making us truly "one flesh" with our mate!

How can we ever be faithful to the living God throughout all eternity if we selfishly refuse to be faithful to the mate to whom we are bound in this life for only a few years and fail to learn the lessons of patience, kindness, long-suffering, self-control, love and faithfulness in the sacred marriage union?

The Teaching of Jesus Christ

Now it becomes increasingly clear why Jesus Christ taught the enduring quality of the marriage vow.

When Jesus was asked by the hypocritical Pharisees why Moses allowed divorce in Old Testament times, He answered: "Moses because of the hardness of your hearts suffered you to put away your wives: but from the beginning it was not so. And I say unto you, Whosoever shall put away his wife, *except it be for fornication*, and shall marry another, committeth adultery: and whoso marrieth her which is put away doth commit adultery" (Matt. 19:8-9).

Divorce generates divorce! A moment's reflection will recall that the commonplace granting of divorces was absolutely unheard of only fifty years ago. The religious leaders of that time and before warned us that if divorce were once tolerated, there would be no restraint powerful enough to keep it within the limits then fixed or foreseen. Today we see the truth of this warning! We now behold the sad and miserable spectacle of marriage after marriage ending in failure in the divorce courts!

And after divorce, what?

It is a matter of record that most divorced persons seek a second mate, and many find a third or a fourth mate to satisfy a desire which God intended should be satisfied and channeled to and uplifted in the holy and sacred marriage with their first mate—who in most cases is still living at the time of the remarriage.

This is a pitiful spectacle and a national disgrace! Even though God *permits* divorce in certain instances, it is far better for each marriage partner to learn to help and serve and *forgive* the other, and thus preserve the sacred marriage bond.

Jesus' famous exception clause, "except it be for fornication [*porneia*]" (Matt. 19:9), should be employed *only* as a last resort and even then after much prayer, counsel, and sincere attempts to save the marriage. And the same would apply to the apostle Paul's permission for the Christian to remarry if *deserted* by an unconverted mate (I Cor. 7:15).

Marriage Is Ordained of God

We now see that marriage is not something that just evolved through the reasoning and gradual civilization of man. Rather, marriage was ordained by the Creator God. He ordained it as a holy union picturing the everlasting faithfulness between Christ and His Church!

And every form of adultery is so very wrong and evil because marriage is so holy and sacred in the sight of Almighty God. Adultery is not only an offense to the aggrieved husband or wife involved; it is an offense to their home and their children. It is an offense against society—because it strikes at the very *basis* of all decent society. But, most of all, it is an offense against God Himself and against an institution which He has ordained.

In many Western nations today, a God-rejecting society all too often seeks a Hollywood-type romantic ideal in marriage. Thus men and women are subtly encouraged to break the marriage covenant if their selfish, sensual desires are not fulfilled with the wife or husband of their youth. In a "marriage-go-round" society, they fail to learn the basic lessons of character which marriage can and should teach—outgoing concern for their mate, patience, mercy, humility, service and lasting faithfulness. In addition, they fail to consider the suffering and frustration of the children from their original marriage—the irreparable damage done to their lives and minds which will carry over into yet future generations and future marriages.

Truly, even though God *allows* some marriages and homes to be shattered by divorce, it is something our Creator abhors. "For the Lord, the God of Israel, saith that he *hateth* putting away [divorce] . . ." (Mal. 2:16). Again: ". . . the Lord hath been witness between thee and the wife of thy youth, against whom thou hast dealt treacherously: yet is she thy companion, and the wife of thy covenant" (verse 14).

No question, then, that God hates divorce—even though He allows it. To learn the lessons God intends in marriage, true Christians should seek to literally "cleave" to their mates in body, mind and attitude. They should seek earnestly to understand each other—to share freely and joyously their plans, their hopes, their dreams. And, with God's help, they will crush any adulterous and lustful thoughts which present themselves.

The sin of lust is more fully understood when you realize how righteous and holy the proper use of sex in marriage is to Almighty God the Creator. The process of adultery, and the process of divorce and remarriage, usually begin in the heart. Notice how Jesus Christ covered this point in magnifying the law of God and making it holy: "Ye have heard that it was said by them of old time, Thou shalt not commit adultery: but I say unto you, That whosoever LOOKETH on a woman *to lust after her* hath committed *adultery* with her already in his heart" (Matt. 5:27-28).

Jesus taught that you break the seventh commandment when you even so much as entertain thoughts of sexual lust toward another person. Action follows thought. So it is part of the development of Christian character for every God-fearing person to learn to guide and to channel his thoughts away from all lust and illicit desires.

Meanwhile, in the industries that control the most realistic, lifelike media that influence and move young people to action—movies and television—the emphasis in an ever increasing number of productions has been upon sex or violence, or a combination of both.

But modern society is paying a terrible penalty for these widespread sins and abominations! More and more homes are made miserable and wretched because of adulterous relations of one or both mates. Increasing numbers of homes are broken in divorce. More children are being left without the love and guidance of both parents! And illicit sexual intercourse before marriage—called "fornication" by God—is becoming epidemic among young people in today's society.

Yet any and all of these things constitute breaking the seventh commandment!

Those young people who are cheapening and damaging the happiness of their future marriages through illicit sex before marriage are seriously injuring their entire future in this present life. And unless they repent and stop this vile practice, they will force God by an eternal necessity to exclude them from His Kingdom and everlasting life and happiness (I Corinthians 6:9). God's laws are always for our own good and the good of those around us. They should be obeyed. We should fear being counted with the "abominable" and "whoremongers" who will have their part in the lake of fire which is the second death! (Revelation 21:8.)

Obey the Seventh Commandment

God gives some important advice to those who are tempted to commit fornication or adultery. In this age of sex stimulation and lust, it is invaluable to HEED this advice if you would enter into the Kingdom of God and eternal life. God says: *"Flee fornication"* (I Cor. 6:18). He does not say to let your mind dwell on wrong sexual ideas or desires. He does not say to place yourself alone with another person's mate or with a single person with whom you might be sexually tempted. He does not say to watch movies or television or read books which wrongly stimulate the sexual appetite.

God does say to get as far away from these things as you possibly can! He says to run—to flee—away from temptation to sexual sin. Sex is not a toy to be played with and experimented with. It should be regarded as a God-given blessing in the holy and sacred marriage union which the Creator Himself has ordained. It should always be thought of with reverence, and as an expression of unselfish love in a Christian union which pictures the everlasting faithfulness of Christ and His Church!

This generation needs desperately to learn the lesson of lasting faithfulness in marriage and in the home! It needs to obey both the letter and the spirit of God's seventh commandment: "Thou shalt not commit adultery."

THE EIGHTH COMMANDMENT

AFTER the God of heaven thundered from the top of Mount Sinai the commandments ordaining the true worship of Him, and laws protecting the most sacred human relationships—the home, the family, and human life itself—God gave the eighth commandment. This is God's law protecting all private property and possessions: "Thou shalt not steal" (Ex. 20:15).

Because men do not think the God who gave this commandment is real—and do not fear to disobey His law—we have more literal theft than ever before. But we also violate the eighth commandment in hundreds of ways through a watered down system of morality.

After discussing some debased scheme by which to cheat a business competitor or customer, executives shrug their shoulders and say: "Well, that's just business." Or, after a meeting involving false measurement, poor quality or misleading advertising, a businessman will say: "What's the difference? If I don't do it, somebody else will." When cheating the government or falsifying an income tax return, the commonly used phrase to salve one's conscience is: "Let the government sweat this time. They're taking too much money anyway. So what?"

Yes, so what? Is that "just business"?

Well, it also happens to be God's business—and He has

set in motion a law stating: "Thou shalt not steal." When you break God's law—it breaks you! For God's laws are living, active things—like the law of gravity. When you transgress them, the punishment is automatic—and it is sure.

The Right to Property

According to God's Word and His law, there are only two right ways by which you can come into possession of anything. The first is by a free gift—or an inheritance—from another person, or from God Himself. The second is by honest labor, which earns something as a legitimate return. Any other way is theft—the taking from another that which belongs to him.

The eighth commandment recognizes the legitimate acquisition of property, and forbids theft. It is important to note that, in principle, the eighth commandment forbids all forms of communism which deny man's right to property. It also forbids international thievery in which governments forcibly confiscate and steal the property and possessions of their own or other nations' citizens. And, to our lasting shame, *all* nations stand guilty of breaking God's law in this respect!

People today are learning to steal in an immensely large and organized fashion. Not only are they purloining articles by the thousands from stores, shops, schools and even churches, but even young people regularly organize an intricate system of cheating on tests and exams in schools and colleges.

Because it is generally looked on without too much alarm, this practice is growing at an unprecedented rate. But what the young people may not have been told is that cheating is taking a score or grade illegally—and is stealing. It is directly breaking the eighth commandment of God!

The industrialist or merchant who uses false weights and measures or a poor quality of material or workmanship to deceive the public is just as guilty of breaking the eighth commandment as a common thief! He is trying to get something more than a legitimate return for his product. Viewing the illegal profits he hopes to receive, he is trying to get that extra something for nothing. In principle, he is simply stealing! Yet, in how many thousands of cases this type of lawlessness and deception is practiced, God alone knows.

Thievery Through Misleading Advertising

One of the great commercial sins of our age is the common practice of misleading advertising. The consumer is led to expect that a certain "pill," for instance, will cause him to lose weight, gain weight, increase his potency, restore his thinning hair, or whatever the case may be. And, in most cases, this statement is a complete distortion without any doubt.

Such a practice is, in effect, stealing from the people who pay money to achieve the promised result.

In many cases, the victims of these gigantic frauds are not only robbed of money, they are robbed of health, happiness and peace of mind. Many a "respectable" businessman and community leader has attained his position largely through this type of mass deception and theft!

Our nations and peoples need to wake up! Just because a sin can be made outwardly to appear "respectable," remember that God is the real Judge.

The Almighty has this to say: "Know ye not that the unrighteous shall not inherit the kingdom of God? Be not deceived: neither fornicators . . . nor thieves . . . shall inherit the kingdom of God" (I Cor. 6:9-10).

Lest any misunderstand, remember that it is God's will that His servants prosper in material wealth—as long as they gain it honestly, and don't set their hearts upon it. The apostle John wrote: "Beloved, I wish above all things that thou mayest prosper and be in health, even as thy soul prospereth" (III John 2).

Tarnished Wealth

Moreover, we must realize that an industrialist's wealth which is tarnished by an unnecessarily high death rate in his plants or factories is ill-gotten gain—and he is branded in the light of God's law as a thief, if not a murderer!

The principle behind the eighth commandment is broken again and again in the relations of capital and labor. James was inspired to warn the dishonest employer: "Behold, the hire of the labourers . . . which is of you kept back by fraud, crieth: and the cries . . . are entered into the ears of the Lord of sabaoth" (Jas. 5:4).

It is also equally true—and especially so in this era of corrupt unionism—that many a workingman robs his employer! He does this by taking his wage and yet withholding his full share of honest labor. And that is stealing!

The eighth commandment of Almighty God has a message for both capital and labor. To capital: "A fair day's wage for a fair day's work." To labor: "A fair day's work for a fair day's wage."

But just stealing from a fellow human being is not the only principle involved in the eighth commandment. God owns far more property than any man (Haggai. 2:8).

Stealing From God

In Malachi 3, speaking to modern-day Jacob or Israel (verse 6), God declares: "Will a man rob God? Yet ye have robbed me. But ye say, Wherein have we robbed thee? In *tithes* and *offerings*" (verse 8). God here indicts our modern English-speaking peoples for robbing our very Creator and His Work! No wonder there is so little true religion left on earth today! No wonder there is so much confusion and deceit going about in the name of Christianity!

God continues: "Ye are cursed with a curse: for ye have robbed me, even this whole nation." Then God promises in His Word: "Bring ye all the *tithes* into the storehouse, that there may be meat in mine house, and *prove me now herewith,* saith the Lord of hosts, if I will not open you the windows of heaven, and pour you out a *blessing*, that there shall not be room enough to receive it" (verses 9-10).

Here is a bold challenge from Almighty God!

God says He will bless you if you begin tithing—as He commands—through faith in Him and in His Word. Literally hundreds of case histories may be cited to show that God certainly does bless the tither even in material ways. He may not always do so immediately. You may have to obey Him and exercise faith for a while. But as you serve Him, obey Him, trust Him, God will keep His part of the bargain. Your blessing is certain to come!

Notice this joyful letter from one who took God's promise literally: "A few weeks ago I was absolutely broke financially. I received ten cents. I was tempted not to tithe the one cent. I did. Then a few days later I received one dollar. Again, I was tempted to keep the tithe because of many needs. I just received forty dollars and am getting the tithe off to you as soon as possible. I have been faithful and so has God."

The Command Applied Positively

The definite positive application of the eighth commandment is stated in the New Testament letter to the Ephesians. "Let him that stole steal no more: but rather let him labour, working with his hands the thing which is good, that he may have to give to him that needeth" (Eph. 4:28). On the one hand, stealing is condemned in this passage. On the other, working and giving are outlined as the way of life the positive application of God's command dictates.

Property and possessions are to be gained by honest work—not merely to satisfy personal desires and needs, but so that any excess may be freely given to the brother in need. In the real intent or spirit of God's law, a man not only steals by taking from another that which is his, but by refusal to work in order to share and give to others in need! The true Christian should be "distributing to the necessity of saints; given to hospitality" (Rom. 12:13). As God's begotten children, we are to become like Him (Matthew 5:48). And Jesus said: "My Father *worketh* hitherto, and I *work*" (John 5:17).

The *positive* lesson of the eighth commandment is also summarized in these all-inclusive words of Jesus, the Christ: "It is more blessed to *give* than to receive" (Acts 20:35). If, through God's Spirit, we can truly learn to live by those words, we will have indeed fulfilled the spirit of the eighth commandment!

THE NINTH COMMANDMENT

THIS is the age of the sophisticated lie, the double standard of morality. The Christ of the Bible thoroughly condemned the hypocrites of His day. What would He say about our generation?

In his book, *Sex, Vice and Business,* Monroe Fry tells of "the willingness of communities to accept vice when it brings an indirect profit to their respectable businessmen."

In plain language, they are living a lie! The revelation of how much our entire "Christian" society is based on this type of hypocrisy is absolutely astounding! But we are paying a stern penalty nevertheless—for we are breaking the ninth commandment of God.

The Ninth Commandment Stated

"Thou shalt not bear false witness against thy neighbour" (Ex. 20:16). It is only in seeking and bearing witness to the truth that man is associated with God. For, in literal fact, God is truth! Jesus said: "Thy word is truth" (John 17:17). And again: "I am the way, the truth, and the life" (John 14:6).

No matter what other faults and weaknesses a man may have, if he is willing to speak the truth, live openly and truthfully what he really is, and acknowledge the truth when it is shown to him, that man can be respected and helped to overcome his personal weaknesses.

The far-reaching spiritual applications of the ninth commandment are tremendous. Consider: 1) There is a personal, living Almighty God of this universe whose ways and laws are intrinsically right. 2) Therefore, a man who is honest, who is willing to speak the truth and acknowledge the truth when it is revealed, must eventually be converted to the true God and His ways! But a man whose word is no good, who is in the habit of lying to others and to himself—that man's very character and mental processes are so twisted and perverted that he can *never* come to understand even the truth of God until his mind is literally cleaned up!

That is why it is so vitally important that—even though among humans there may be honest differences of opinion on many matters—we all learn to live and speak truthfully. Yet, we are living in a society which is increasingly permeated by various forms of untruth, hypocrisy and self-deception. If we are ever to build the character of God—and inherit eternal life—we must consider the ninth commandment in all of its ramifications—and learn to obey it.

The ninth commandment protects every upright and decent man in that it helps guard his reputation. Perhaps there is no more despicable sin than that of slander, the lie invented and spread abroad with intent to harm one's fellowman. A thief takes only material goods, which may usually be replaced. But a false witness who slanders may rob one of esteem and reputation in the eyes of his fellowmen—and chances are slim that it will ever be fully regained.

The Practical Value of Honesty

The immediate value of being able to rely on a man's word would not only guard every decent man's reputation and eliminate millions of wasted hours from the burden of investigating every statement and report several times over, it would also prevent unworthy men from ever being placed in high positions of responsibility. It would literally clean up our society!

In the field of industry and business, think of the tremendous benefit that would come to the public if each company would really tell the truth about its own product and honestly seek to serve the consumer's real needs! The effects of this would be literally astounding! Think of a society where each brand of toothpaste and breakfast cereal, for example, was not just an imitation or needless variation of another but was the only and best of its particular type, honestly priced and truthfully advertised! Apply this to every phase of society and you get something near utopia.

But this is not a farfetched or fantastic suggestion. It is simply the blessing that would come if the entire society really and literally obeyed the ninth commandment of God!

If you would live forever in the society of God, you are commanded by Him who gives you life and breath: "Wherefore putting away lying, speak every man truth with his neighbour: for we are members one of another" (Eph. 4:25).

Apply the Ninth Commandment in Your Life

The very root principle of all sin is vanity. "Vanity of vanities, saith the Preacher, vanity of vanities; all is vanity" (Eccl. 1:2). The real reason most men reject the true God is that they want to be "gods" in their own eyes and the eyes of their fellowmen. It is vanity. Every sin that is committed by man has its ultimate roots in this one principle. And so it is with every form of lying. Men lie because they are more concerned with their own self-esteem and sense of importance than they are with the ultimate good of their fellowman. They speak and act falsely because they fear the opinions of men much more than that of Almighty God Himself! The daily actions and words of nearly all men bear eloquent testimony to the literal truth of this statement.

As John said even of the religious leaders of his day: "For they loved the praise of men more than the praise of God" (John 12:43). Men and women are often ashamed of what they call "failure" in a business or social sense. They will cheat, falsify and lie in order to avoid this "failure"—or to cover it up. But from the point of view of what is intrinsically "right"—and of eternal values—the thing they should fear is sin. For, as the apostle Paul said, "If God be for us, who can be against us?" (Rom. 8:31.)

Jesus said: "Blessed are ye, when men shall revile you, and persecute you, and shall speak all manner of evil against you falsely, for my sake" (Matt. 5:11). We had all better quit worrying so much about what puny, mortal men think—and become far more concerned about what Almighty God thinks! Then we will learn to cease from all hypocrisy in business, in social life, in politics—yes, in our religious and scientific endeavors.

Remember that many whom this deceitful world condemned have received God's blessing and are heirs of eternal life. Never forget that it was through the sin of false testimony and lying that Jesus Christ was murdered! "For many bare false witness against him, but their witness agreed not together" (Mark 14:56).

Since, through vanity, men want to believe what is popular at the moment, they will kid themselves and their associates into believing even religious and scientific theories that have no basis whatsoever in actual fact!

God warns against all such hypocrites: "For the wrath of God is revealed from heaven against all ungodliness and unrighteousness of men, who hold the truth in unrighteousness" (Rom. 1:18). Most Bible commentaries or lexicons show that the expression "hold" should have been translated "hold down" or "suppress." Men *suppress* the truth.

God is condemning those who knowingly hold down or suppress the truth of His existence and His purpose on this earth! God says the vain philosophers and scientists of this world are "without excuse" for denying that He literally created this universe and is now ruling it through His power (verse 20). Most scientists and theologians who believe in the Satan-inspired theory of evolution ought to know better. Some of them do know better! But they are going along with what pleases men, and they are living a lie! God says they are "without excuse"!

And in the same category are those ministers and Bible students who continue to teach and practice what they know are ancient heathen and pagan beliefs and customs condemned in the Word of God. In all too many cases, they know better! They are "without excuse."

The continued teaching of these basic scientific and spiritual lies is the very thing that is blinding most of this world from the real nature of God and of His true plan and purpose here below. This is the truly terrible result of bearing false witness, self-deception and lying. For as long as supposedly "educated" leaders keep deceiving themselves and others about the very existence and power and plan of God, our civilization is doomed!

Live by the Truth

In your own personal life, then, learn the importance of telling the truth, believing the truth, living the truth. Be careful not to base your whole life on a series of lies—whether they be personal, political, scientific or religious distortions of truth. Remember, it is the real truth which will make you free (John 8:32).

In your personal speech, guard your words carefully. Never forget that a man is only as good as his word. If a man becomes an habitual liar, it is almost impossible to help him—for anything he says or does may simply be another deception.

One of the basic qualities of God's character is that He is truth. If we couldn't rely on God's Word, there could be no real assurance of forgiveness from past sins, of present help in time of need, or of future reward and eternal life.

Even though God had tremendous well-meaning love, and all wisdom and power—but you couldn't rely on His Word or His promises—where would you be?

Have you ever thought of it that way before?

The very diametric opposite of God's character is that of Satan the devil. As Jesus Christ revealed: "When he speaketh a lie, he speaketh of his own: *for he is a liar*, and the father of it" (John 8:44). Those who follow Satan in his refusal to live by truth have a terrible fate awaiting them: "But the fearful, and unbelieving . . . and *all liars*, shall have their part in the lake which burneth with fire and brimstone: which is the second death" (Rev. 21:8).

Remember, there are no "white lies" in God's sight. Half-truths, distortions and deceptions are condemned throughout God's Word. Jesus said: "Thy word *is truth*" (John 17:17). Let us live by that inspired Word that we may inherit eternal life in the kingdom that is based on what is literally true and right. This is the message of the ninth commandment.

THE TENTH COMMANDMENT

DID you know that the financial troubles plaguing most families are not the result of low income? Rather, they are directly caused by overextending a normally adequate income for luxuries and personal indulgence, and by the Western habit of installment buying!

"Buy now and pay later," say the advertisements.

But do you really need to buy this item now? And are you sure you will be able to "pay later"?

A Society Based on Lust

"Keeping up with the Joneses" is a popular American slogan. High-pressure advertisements constantly encourage this idea. It is made to seem backward or wrong not to strive and compete and lust after as many material possessions as your neighbor owns. The modern idea is to "get all you can while the getting is good."

The incessant pressure to get ahead—which usually means to acquire more money and material property—has spawned more and more idolatry. It is blinding the minds and hearts of millions to the life of God.

Several years ago, a prominent religious publication, *The Canadian Churchman,* ran a sobering article revealing the effect of this material idolatry on young African Christians studying in the United States and Canada. One such young man said: "Before I came to study here, I was a good Christian. I dreamed someday of becoming a medical missionary. Now I'm an atheist."

"Why?" asked the shocked interviewer.

"Since coming here," he replied, "I've discovered that the white man has two gods. One that he taught us about, and another one to whom he prays. A Presbyterian mission school taught me that the tribal doctrines of my ancestors who worshiped images and believed in witchcraft were wrong and almost ludicrous. But here you worship larger images—cars and electrical appliances. I honestly can't see the difference."

We live in a society which is literally based on lust and greed for more and more material things! The frenzied effort to compete with others and get ahead is the source not only of most financial problems, but the real cause of much physical and mental illness, broken homes, frustrated lives. Most important of all, this form of idolatry leaves one with almost no time, strength or desire ever to become acquainted with the true God—whose living laws and ways alone would bring real inner peace and joy.

The Tenth Commandment Stated

Most men fail to realize that the Ten Commandments are living, moving, active laws—like the law of gravity. They are automatic. When you break them, they break you! So it is with the final commandment of God's law. Even though it may be broken without the knowledge of any other human being, the penalty for its violation is absolutely certain!

"Thou shalt not covet thy neighbour's house, thou shalt not covet thy neighbour's wife, nor his manservant, nor his maidservant, nor his ox, nor his ass, nor any thing that is thy neighbour's" (Ex. 20:17).

Of all the commandments, the tenth refers most specifically to man's relation to man. The force of the commandment lies in these words: "Thy neighbour's . . . thy neighbour's . . . his . . . his . . . his . . . his . . . thy neighbour's." This is a *sevenfold* guarding of the interests of another.

It is not wrong to lawfully desire a wife, a servant, or an ox or ass. But where the object admired is legitimately out of reach of the one admiring, admiration merging into desire to possess breaks the commandment.

Although this commandment deals most obviously with human and physical relationships, the *spiritual requirement* of the command is in some ways more rigid than any that has preceded it. This command regulates even the thoughts in the mind and heart of man.

Most people look on sin as an outward or physical type of thing. They do not realize that the holy, righteous character which God purposes in us necessitates that even our thoughts be completely purified and made like His. Action follows thought. What you think, you are.

If you secretly reject God's standard and His way, if in your heart you lust after something which you either cannot or will not come to lawfully possess with His blessing, then—sooner or later—this mental rebellion will bring forth outward sin. The actions will then proceed to defy God—to break His law—because the thoughts have been doing this all along!

This command pierces through all "surface Christianity" and shows whether a man has really surrendered his will to his Maker! It is a searching and fearful principle. But it is a command you must learn to obey if you are ever to receive eternal life and glory in the kingdom of God.

"Let this mind be in you, which was also in Christ Jesus" (Phil. 2:5). Through God's Spirit in us, we must fight the fight of faith—put down the lustful human nature within us—and ultimately succeed in "bringing into captivity every thought to the obedience of Christ" (II Cor. 10:5). This is the ultimate goal of the true Christian—to be fully attained in the resurrection.

But we are to grow in God's character during this life. We must learn, as did righteous Enoch, Noah, Abraham and other servants of the Most High, to "walk with God." We must go His way—do as He does—think as He thinks.

But the normal mind of man is filled with selfishness, vanity, competition, greed, hate, lust. It is a mind cut off from the ways and thoughts of God (Isaiah 55:8, 9).

That is why Jesus emphasized how important it is to get our minds changed, converted and cleaned up when He said:

"Blessed are the pure in heart: for they shall see God" (Matt. 5:8).

Where Do We Stand?

Especially since World War II has life in our Western society speeded up. We have been rushing to make more money. We have been in a hurry to have a good time, to get everything we can out of life. On every side, we have been taught to compete with our fellowman for social honors and material advancement. We have come to literally crave material luxuries that were in some cases completely unknown just two generations ago.

We have been urged to spend more than we make—to do more than we ought. "You owe it to yourself," the subtle advertisement reads in putting over the idea that we would be foolish not to buy a bigger car, eat at a more expensive restaurant, or take longer and more costly trips. The emphasis is on getting and on self.

On an international scale, the nations of the world fight and kill because of this same attitude of heart. "From whence come wars and fightings among you? come they not hence, even of your lusts that war in your members? Ye lust, and have not: ye kill, and desire to have, and cannot obtain: ye fight and war, yet ye have not, because ye ask not" (Jas. 4:1-2).

All too often, the capitalist lusts for more money than he can easily attain by paying fair wages. So he robs his employees by paying too little, and spending too little on improving working conditions and safety. Likewise, the modern laborer—often misguided by unscrupulous union leaders—learns to lust after more money than he can honestly earn. Through organized pressure and political trickery, he thinks he can get something for nothing.

Why do so-called "authors" write cheap paperback novels based on nothing but filth, obscenity and juvenile stupidity? Why do publishers print such corruption which degrades the human emotions of love, kindness and idealism to a level lower than the dumb brute?

You can quickly see *hundreds* of other major examples of covetousness in our society if your eyes are really open.

But be willing to see your own covetousness as well! Be willing to repent of it and ask God for the love and strength to overcome it.

Our generation needs these words of the Son of God: "Take heed, and beware of covetousness: for a man's life consisteth not in the abundance of the things which he possesseth" (Luke 12:15).

Did you get that? Your real success and happiness in life, Christ said, is not truly able to be measured by how new or powerful a car you drive, the kind of home you live in, the clothes you wear, or even the food you eat. Happiness is a state of mind. It comes from having the very Spirit and mind of Christ inside your own mind. Paul said: ". . . I have learned in whatsoever state I am, therewith to be content" (Phil. 4:11). The love, joy and peace which Jesus exemplified came from giving and serving—not from any material thing Jesus was able to get.

Jesus, the Son of man, was able to overcome human vanity and covetousness because He put the service of God far ahead of anything and everything else. After telling how the unconverted seek after—and worry about—the material necessities and comforts, He commanded: "But seek ye first the kingdom of God, and his righteousness; and all these things shall be added unto you" (Matt. 6:33).

The Commandments Join Together

And so at this point the last commandment joins hands with the first. For whatever you seek contrary to God's will, you covet. If in your mind and heart you lust and covet something more than to obey the Creator and receive His blessings, that thing becomes an idol to you. "Covetousness . . . *is* idolatry" (Col. 3:5).

Then, whatever you idolize you put in place of the true God. And you break the first commandment: "Thou shalt have no other gods before me" (Ex. 20:3). The apostle Paul, concerned about this near-universal sin, said: "Know ye not, that to whom ye yield yourselves servants to obey, his servant ye are to whom ye obey; whether of sin unto death, or of obedience unto righteousness?" (Rom. 6:16.)

When you begin to covet material things, you "serve"

them. You spend your time, your energy, your money for these things.

In such a situation, you have neither time nor energy to really study the Bible, or to spend an hour in earnest prayer before the One who gives you life and breath. And you find yourself being stingy and jealous of the money you owe your Maker to finance the proclamation of His truth. By this simple process, the material things you lust for and covet literally become your god. For you truly serve and worship them—and find in your life little time, strength and wealth with which to serve the true God with all of your heart, strength and mind.

Do you see?

Covetousness is a terrible thing—for it cuts you off from the fellowship and blessings and love of the great God of heaven who made all that is—and intended that this material creation be used in His service and for His glory. And, in practical daily life, covetousness violates the basic principle of the way of life set forth by all the commandments of God and by Jesus Christ Himself.

Jesus summarized this principle of giving as one's motivation, instead of getting, when He said: "It is more blessed to give *than to receive*" (Acts 20:35).

In learning to lovingly, sincerely and intelligently serve your fellowman, and to serve and worship the true God, you will find the only real sense of fulfillment and joy in this life. And in the world tomorrow, you will be given eternal life and glory in a divine government literally based on the Ten Commandments—the true way of love, of giving and serving your fellowman, and of worshiping and exalting the living God who gave these commandments for our eternal good.

THE NEW COMMANDMENTS OF JESUS

THIS is an age of REBELLION against all law and constituted authority. Nations and governments are being overthrown, and homes and schools thrown into chaos by various forms of rebellion.

A revealing insight into modern man's reaction to the phrase in the Lord's Prayer "Thy kingdom come, Thy will be done" was given by a minister.

He wrote: "We do not mean it. *We don't like authority,* nor will we give in easily even if He is the King of heaven . . . It is all too obvious that most men over most of the years have prayed earnestly: 'Thy kingdom *not* come, *my* will be done.' "

Ten Commandments Abolished?

But today, many professing ministers and Bible teachers are proclaiming that the Ten Commandments are either "done away"—as they say—or replaced by the "new" commandments of Jesus.

What are these "new" commandments? Do they replace or contradict the Ten Commandments? What does the Bible reveal on this important subject?

First of all, let us notice one of the all-important purposes for Jesus Christ's coming to this earth in the human flesh. Isaiah prophesied of Jesus: "He will magnify the law and make it honourable" (Isa. 42:21). Here we find that Christ came not to abolish the law, but to magnify it. Magnify has just the opposite meaning of changing or abolishing something. It means to reveal in minute detail, to enlarge upon. Certainly the life and teachings of Jesus do just that with the Father's law.

Jesus said: "Think NOT that I am come to destroy the law, or the prophets: I am *not* come to destroy, but to fulfill" (Matt. 5:17).

Jesus did just what these words imply. Both in His life and teaching, He fulfilled the law. He magnified it by His perfect example. He *filled it to the full,* passing beyond the mere letter to observe even the minutest spiritual intent and purpose of the Father's perfect law.

Those who knew Him as a teacher could never charge Him with having substituted the traditions of men for the commandments of God. He OBEYED the Ten Commandments in word and in deed. He taught and lived them as the perfect way of life.

He said: "Whosoever therefore shall break one of these least commandments, and shall teach men so, he shall be called the least in the kingdom of heaven: but whosoever shall do and teach them, the same shall be called great in the kingdom of heaven" (Matt. 5:19).

The Way to Eternal Life

When a young man came to Jesus Christ asking the way to eternal life, Jesus said: "If thou wilt enter into life, *keep the commandments*" (Matt. 19:16-18). The young man asked, "Which?"

And Jesus answered: "Thou shalt do no murder, Thou shalt not commit adultery . . ." and proceeded to list a number of the Ten Commandments.

Jesus Christ knew the way to salvation! He said that way was obedience to the law of God the Father and surrender to His will.

Jesus declared: "Not every one that saith unto me, Lord, Lord, shall enter into the Kingdom of heaven; but he that *doeth the* WILL of my Father which is in heaven" (Matt. 7:21). Far from abolishing the Ten Commandments, Jesus obeyed them (John 15:10). Christ was the "light" that God sent into the world to show men *HOW* to live.

After His death and resurrection, Christ sent the apostles out with this command: "Go ye therefore, and teach all nations, baptizing them in the name of the Father, and of the Son, and of the Holy Spirit: teaching them to observe ALL THINGS whatsoever I have *commanded* you" (Matt. 28:18-20).

The apostles had been there when Christ told the young man: "Keep the commandments." They had heard Him magnify the commandments of God in what is called the Sermon on the Mount (Matt. 5, 6, 7).

The apostles had witnessed the obedience of Christ to the Ten Commandments, and knew that His was the perfect example. Therefore, when Jesus Christ sent them out to every nation with the order to teach them all things He had commanded them, there could be no possible doubt in their minds but that this included the Ten Commandments of God. Obedience to the Ten Commandments, then, was the very basis of the teaching of Christ and of His original apostles.

But what about the "new" commandments of Jesus? Did they not alter or abolish the necessity for literally keeping the Ten Commandments that were revealed in the Old Testament?

A "New" Commandment

Actually, in spite of what many think, there is only one place in all the Bible where Jesus said he was giving a "new" commandment. The other references—by the apostle John—are to the exact same principles, as we shall see.

"A new commandment I give unto you, that ye love one another; *as* I have loved you, that ye also love one another. By this shall all men know that ye are my disciples, if ye have love one to another" (John 13:34-35).

Jesus gave this "new" commandment the last night of His physical life on earth. He had—by teaching and example—already shown the disciples that keeping God's commandments was simply an expression of love.

Christ had already summarized God's law into the two great principles: "Thou shalt love the Lord thy God with all thy heart, and with all thy soul, and with all thy mind... Thou shalt love thy neighbour as thyself" (Matt. 22:37-39).

In fact, the latter part of this summary of God's law Jesus quoted directly from the Old Testament (Lev. 19:18).

What, then, was "new" about Jesus' command to love our neighbors? The answer is plain. The principle of loving our neighbors was not new, but Jesus' *magnification* of that principle in His own perfect life shed a completely new light on the spiritual intent and depth of this commandment.

Remember Jesus' emphasis—"AS *I have loved you,* that ye also love one another."

Jesus' own perfect example of love and service was the greatest and most meaningful magnification of the love of neighbor as commanded by God. In His life, He demonstrated how that love actually functions in day-to-day life.

How to Love Your Neighbor

Three times the Divine voice broke the usual silence of the heavens in announcing the satisfaction of God in the life of Jesus. Even the Roman Procurator, Pontius Pilate, declared: "I find no fault in Him" (John 19:4).

This was because Jesus lived a life of giving to others. Whether in His constant teaching of the multitudes, His healing of the sick, His feeding of the hungry crowds or in an act of humility such as washing the disciples' feet, He was always giving of Himself.

"Ye serpents, ye generation of vipers, how can ye escape the damnation of hell?" (Matt. 23:33).

Are these strange words from a man of love? No. Rather, they are manifestation of how perfect love sometimes says and does things for the good of others which at the time they may not appreciate.

Jesus loved these Pharisees! It was in love that He thundered these words to wake them up from a life of religious hypocrisy and perversity that was damning them to the lake of fire. Remember, it was also for these same Pharisees that Jesus died. It was for these men and others like them that Jesus prayed: "Father, forgive them: for they know not what they do" (Luke 23:34).

It was in that perfect, understanding love that Jesus

withdrew Himself occasionally from the multitude to rest, to meditate, to pray. For He knew that only by keeping close to the Father and being an instrument in His hands could His human presence and teaching enrich the lives of others.

Jesus did not just act like He loved others. He did love them with a perfect love. Through God's Holy Spirit within Him, He desired from the heart to love and serve His fellow beings for their highest good.

He literally lived the words Paul later showed He uttered: "It is more blessed to *give* than to receive" (Acts 20:35). In this way, His command that men love one another "even as I have loved you," certainly does become a "new" and more all-encompassing command in governing human relationships.

Did Jesus LITERALLY Obey the Ten Commandments?

Many religious folk think that Jesus had a sentimental type of "love" in His heart, but that He didn't really obey God's commandments literally.

The truth is that Jesus Christ kept and obeyed every one of the Ten Commandments in the letter and in the Spirit—just as His followers today should do. As we have already seen, He declared that He had obeyed the Father's commandments (John 15:10).

To make it perfectly clear, Jesus Christ never had another god before the true God. He never committed idolatry, or blasphemed God's name. Jesus *kept holy* the Sabbath that God had made holy and often worshipped in the synagogue on that day as was His custom (Luke 4:16).

Jesus honoured His parents, and He never killed, committed adultery, stole, lied or coveted. He set us an EXAMPLE that we should follow in His steps (I Pet. 2:21).

Today, a true Christian is one so surrendered to God that Christ is actually living *His* life in that person through the indwelling power of the Holy Spirit.

For the apostle Paul said: "I am crucified with Christ: nevertheless I live; yet not I, but CHRIST LIVETH IN ME: and the life I now live in the flesh I live by the faith of the Son of God, Who loved me, and gave Himself for me" (Gal. 2:20).

A true Christian should not only have faith *in* Christ, but should live by the very faith of Christ placed in him by the Holy spirit. Christ—through the Spirit—should literally be living in the true Christian.

And remember, Christ will live the same life in you today that He did 1900 years ago—setting an example. "Jesus Christ the same yesterday, and today, and forever" (Heb. 13:8).

Jesus, in His flesh, "was in all points tempted like as we are, yet without sin" (Heb. 4:15). Yet in His fleshly life He obeyed the Ten Commandments. Dwelling now in His laborers through the Holy Spirit, He will keep the commandments in them.

It is Christ's love. It is *His* power IN us that can keep the spiritual law of God. For Jesus Christ was, and is, obedient to God the Father.

Did John Give a "New" Commandment?

In the epistle of the apostle Jesus loved, the apostle John, we also find reference to a "new" commandment: "Brethren, I write no new commandment unto you, but an old commandment which ye had from the beginning. The old commandment is the word which ye have heard from the beginning. Again, a NEW commandment I write unto you, which thing is true in him and in you: because the darkness is past and the true light now shineth. He that is in the light, and hateth his brother, is in darkness even until now" (I John 2:7-9).

Here the apostle refers his flock first of all to the "word" of God which they had from the beginning. But then he mentions one "new" thing. He proceeds to explain this is the deep spiritual love which brethren in Christ should have for one another. There is simply no room in this love for hate, envy or malice.

But does this Christian love "do away" or change the Ten Commandments of God? Of course not! It only *emphasizes* and *magnifies* the personal love Christians must have toward their fellow men. This love goes *far beyond* the letter of the Ten Commandments— but by no means *replaces* them!

Again, John wrote in his second epistle: "And now I

beseech thee, lady, not as though I wrote a new commandment unto thee, but that which we had from the beginning, that we love one another. And this is love, that we walk after His commandments. This is the commandment, that as ye have heard from the beginning, ye should walk in it" (II John 5-6).

Here John defines Christian LOVE as *keeping the commandments!*

We are not just to love the persons of God and Christ. We are to love their way—their very character—which is expressed in the Ten Commandments. Christ not only taught obedience to the commandments, He lived them!

And so John adds: "Whosoever transgresseth and abideth not in the doctrine of Christ, hath not God. He that abideth in the doctrine of Christ, he hath both the Father and the Son" (verse 9).

When we examine the positive side of the "new" commandments, we find that they simply reinforce and make more binding the old! They outline a way of love—of giving—of serving, which can only be attained through Christ Himself living in us. In perfect unselfishness, we are to learn to love our fellow man as Jesus loved us.

That is new Testament doctrine! It is FAR MORE binding than the letter of the commandments stated in the Old Testament.

But it does not replace them. Rather, it magnifies them to their full spiritual intent. And these "new" commandments themselves refer to the perfect magnification in the life of Jesus. And Jesus obeyed the Ten Commandments in spirit as well. He is to be our "light," our example.

Describing the principle of how we should love our neighbor, the apostle Paul stated: "Love is the fulfilling of the law" (Rom. 13:10). For God's spiritual love flows down the riverbed, or channel, expressed in the Ten Commandments.

In perfectly obeying the Ten Commandments—in their every phase and facet—Jesus' entire life was a radiant life of love itself, and love is the fulfillment of law.

The "new" commandment He gave called attention to His perfect example of obedience to the Father, and of kindness and service to all men.

Far from "doing away" with God's law, Jesus' life and teaching shows us that *all ten* of God's Commandments should be practiced in the life of every one of us. Though modern man has strayed very far from God, this is what "true Christianity" is all about.

This is the basis of the CHARACTER God wants to build in you before He grants you eternal life.

Do you deeply want eternal life in the soon-coming Kingdom of God? Then don't treat cheaply Jesus' previously noted statement to the young man: "IF thou wilt enter into life, *keep the Commandments*."

A Unique Course Understanding

Have you found it difficult—even impossible—to understand what the Bible says? The Ambassador College Bible Correspondence Course can help you begin to comprehend the Bible as never before. More than 2,000,000 people have enrolled in this unique course!

These informative, eye-opening lessons make plain the answers to the "unanswerable" problems facing millions today. They explain the very purpose of human life. You will study the plain truths of your Bible!

You will learn the truth about the purpose of life, about what Bible prophecy says concerning world events today, about the God-inspired way to true happiness. All these topics and more are presented in step-by-step detail. A different major subject is explored in each monthly lesson.

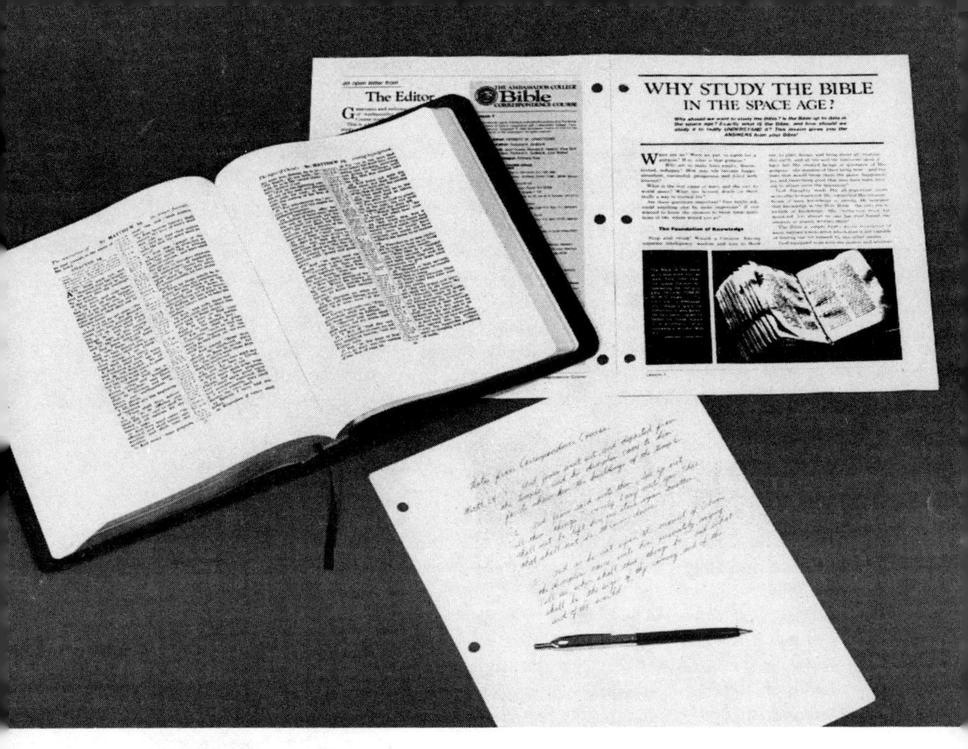

in Bible

And the Bible itself is the only textbook you will need.

You will find each lesson richly rewarding, and periodic quizzes will help you evaluate your progress. There is no tuition fee or obligation—these lessons are absolutely free! Why not request a sample lesson? Send your request in the reply envelope or write to our address nearest you.

Free of Charge

Just mail the reply envelope stitched into this booklet.

MAILING ADDRESSES WORLDWIDE

United States: Worldwide Church of God, Pasadena, California 91123

United Kingdom, Europe (except as listed) and Middle East: The Plain Truth, P.O. Box 111, Borehamwood, Herts, England WD6 1LU

Canada: Worldwide Church of God, P.O. Box 44, Station A, Vancouver, B.C. V6C 2M2

Canada (French language): Le Monde à Venir, B.P. 121, Succ. A, Montreal, P. Q. H3C 1C5

Mexico: Institución Ambassador, Apartado Postal 5-595, 06502 Mexico D.F.

South America: Institución Ambassador, Apartado Aéreo 11430, Bogotá 1, D.E., Colombia

Caribbean: Worldwide Church of God, G.P.O. Box 6063, San Juan, Puerto Rico 00936-6063

France: Le Monde à Venir, B.P. 64, 75662 Paris Cédex 14, France

Switzerland: Le Monde à Venir, Case Postale 10, 91 rue de la Servette, CH-1211 Genève 7, Suisse

Italy: La Pura Verità, Casella Postale 10349 I-00144 Roma EUR, Italia

Germany: Ambassador College, Postfach 1129, D-5300 Bonn 1, West Germany

Holland and Belgium: Ambassador College, Postbus 444, 3430 AK Nieuwegein, Nederland

Belgium: Le Monde à Venir, B.P. 31, 6000 Charleroi 1, Belgique

Denmark: The Plain Truth, Box 211, DK-8100 Aarhus C, Denmark

Norway: The Plain Truth, Postboks 2513 Solli, N-0203 Oslo 2, Norway

Sweden: The Plain Truth, Box 5380, S-102 46, Stockholm, Sweden

Finland: The Plain Truth, Box 603, SF-00101 Helsinki, Finland

Australia: Worldwide Church of God, P.O. Box 202, Burleigh Heads, Queensland 4220, Australia

India: Worldwide Church of God, P.O. Box 6727, Bombay 400 052, India

Sri Lanka: Worldwide Church of God, P.O. Box 1824, Colombo, Sri Lanka

Malaysia: Worldwide Church of God, P.O. Box 430, Jalan Sultan, 46750 Petaling Jaya, Selangor, Malaysia

Singapore: Worldwide Church of God, P.O. Box 111, Farrer Road Post Office, Singapore 9128

New Zealand and the Pacific Isles: Ambassador College, P.O. Box 2709, Auckland 1, New Zealand

The Philippines: Worldwide Church of God, P.O. Box 1111, MCPO, 1299 Makati, Metro Manila, Philippines

Israel: Ambassador College, P.O. Box 19111, Jerusalem

South Africa: Ambassador College, P.O. Box 5644, Cape Town 8000, South Africa

Zimbabwe: Ambassador College, Box UA30, Union Avenue, Harare, Zimbabwe

Nigeria: Worldwide Church of God, PMB 21006, Ikeja, Lagos State, Nigeria

Ghana: Worldwide Church of God, P.O. Box 9617, Kotoka International Airport, Accra, Ghana

Kenya: Worldwide Church of God, P.O. Box 47135, Nairobi, Kenya

Mauritius: The Plain Truth, P.O. Box 888, Port Louis, Mauritius

THIS BOOKLET IS PROVIDED FREE OF CHARGE BY THE WORLDWIDE CHURCH OF GOD IN THE PUBLIC INTEREST. It is made possible by the voluntary, freely given tithes and offerings of the membership of the Church and others who have elected to support the work of the Church. Contributions are welcomed and gratefully accepted. Those who wish to voluntarily aid and support this worldwide Work of God are gladly welcomed as co-workers in this major effort to preach the gospel to all nations.

358797/8902
DELTA